Deep Learning with Rust

Mehrdad Maleki

Deep Learning with Rust

Mastering Efficient and Safe Neural Networks
in the Rust Ecosystem

Apress®

Mehrdad Maleki ⓘ
Naas, Kildare, Ireland

ISBN 979-8-8688-2207-0   ISBN 979-8-8688-2208-7   (eBook)
https://doi.org/10.1007/979-8-8688-2208-7

This Apress imprint is published by the registered company APress Media, LLC, part of Springer Nature.
The registered company address is: 1 New York Plaza, New York, NY 10004, U.S.A.

If disposing of this product, please recycle the paper.

*To my dear wife, **Somi**, for her patience and constant support through every step of this journey.*
*To my dear older son, **Sami**, whose encouragement gave me the strength to finish this book.*
*To my dear little son, **Soren**, for all the moments we missed playing together while I was working—this book is for you, too.*
*And to my dear **parents**, for the love and guidance that shaped who I am. This book is also yours.*

Declarations

Competing Interests The author has no competing interests to declare that are relevant to the content of this manuscript.

Contents

About the Author

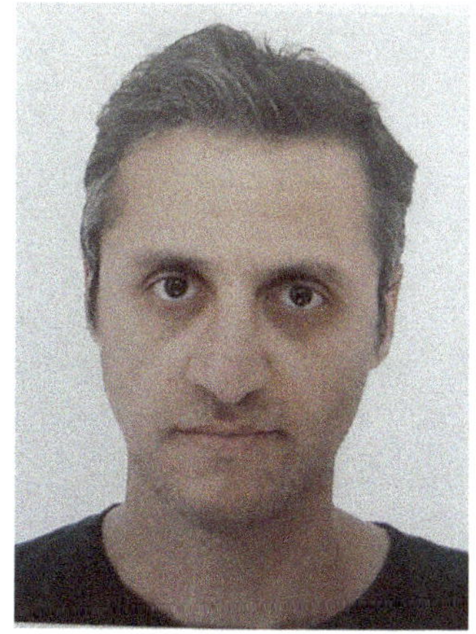

Dr. Mehrdad Maleki holds a Ph.D. in Theoretical Computer Science and a master's degree in Mathematics. He is an accomplished AI scientist and researcher specializing in artificial intelligence, quantum computing, and cybersecurity. His work combines deep mathematical insight with practical engineering to design scalable, high-performance AI and quantum systems.

Over the years, Dr. Maleki has led several R&D projects, contributing to more than ten patents in AI and quantum computing. His research and innovations span areas such as deep learning, foundation models, automatic differentiation, and scientific computing. Proficient in Python and Rust, he bridges the gap between theoretical research and real-world applications by transforming complex algorithms into impactful solutions.

About the Technical Reviewer

Andrew Rzeznik is a Senior Systems Engineer at Cloudflare, working on problems in networking. He has previously done programming work in cryptography, data processing, and factory automation. He holds a Ph.D. in Mathematics from MIT, where his research focused on atmospheric waves and deep-sea mining plumes. In his spare time he enjoys woodworking and being with his family.

Introduction

Artificial Intelligence (AI) and deep learning are among the most transformative technologies of our time. They are reshaping how we live, work, and interact with the world—driving innovations in finance, healthcare, manufacturing, and beyond. However, as deep learning models grow in scale and complexity, so do the challenges of implementing them efficiently, securely, and reliably.

This book, *Deep Learning with Rust,* is written to bridge the gap between **theoretical understanding** and **high-performance implementation**. It combines the mathematical and conceptual foundations of deep learning with the engineering precision of Rust—a modern programming language designed for safety, concurrency, and performance.

By the end of this book, readers will not only understand how deep learning works but also how to build, optimize, and scale deep learning systems in Rust from the ground up.

Who This Book Is For

This book is intended for readers who are curious about how **AI systems work under the hood** and who wish to go beyond using existing libraries. It assumes a basic understanding of programming and mathematics (functions, calculus, and probability) but does not require prior knowledge of Rust or deep learning.

It is particularly useful for:

- **AI practitioners** who want to explore Rust as a new, safer, and faster alternative to Python for implementing deep learning models.
- **Developers and engineers** interested in building efficient and reliable AI systems for production environments.
- **Researchers and students** looking to strengthen their understanding of deep learning fundamentals while learning how to implement them in a high-performance language.

Each chapter is self-contained yet builds progressively toward a comprehensive mastery of the subject.

What This Book Covers

The book is divided into two main parts, designed to take readers from basic concepts to advanced implementations.

- **Part I—Foundations of Deep Learning in Rust** introduces the principles of AI and deep learning, explores why language choice matters for performance and scalability, and shows how to set up a complete Rust environment for AI development. It covers essential Rust syntax, data structures, error handling, ownership, and memory management—all framed from an AI practitioner's perspective.
- **Part II—Advancing with Rust in AI** moves from concepts to practice. It explains how to implement neural networks from scratch, build and train perceptrons, and extend these to more advanced architectures such as **Convolutional Neural Networks (CNNs)**, **Recurrent Neural Networks (RNNs)**, **Long Short-Term Memory (LSTM) networks**, **Generative Adversarial Networks (GANs)**, and **Transformers**.

  Each chapter walks through mathematical derivations, Rust code examples, and visual outputs, helping readers understand both how models work and how to implement them safely and efficiently.

Throughout the book, you will also learn about **automatic differentiation**, **concurrency and parallelism**, and **optimization workflows**, all within the Rust ecosystem.

How to Use This Book

This book combines theory, code, and exercises.

Each chapter begins with a clear conceptual explanation, followed by annotated examples in Rust and practice problems at the end.

To get the most out of it:

- Work through the examples interactively.
- Modify the code, experiment with parameters, and observe how changes affect the output.
- Review the **Problems** sections to reinforce learning.
- Access the **companion GitHub repository**, which includes all source code, exercises, and updates aligned with the latest version of Rust and its machine learning crates.

This hands-on approach ensures that readers gain not only theoretical knowledge but also practical skills that can be applied directly in AI projects.

Why Rust for Deep Learning?

While most deep learning frameworks today are written in Python, performance-critical components are implemented in C++ or CUDA. Rust offers a unified alternative: the **speed of C**, the **safety of memory ownership**, and the **expressiveness of a modern language**.

Rust's features—such as strict compile-time checks, zero-cost abstractions, and safe concurrency—make it ideal for building scalable AI systems that avoid the pitfalls of memory leaks, segmentation faults, and data races.

In addition, the Rust ecosystem has rapidly matured with crates like ndarray, linfa, and tch, which enable high-level AI development while maintaining low-level control.

Rust empowers developers to write **fast, safe, and energy-efficient AI code**, making it a compelling choice for the next generation of AI research and production.

Final Thoughts

The journey through this book is both technical and conceptual. It starts with understanding what deep learning is and ends with implementing advanced models capable of solving real-world problems. Along the way, you will gain insight into how AI systems think, learn, and adapt—and how to translate those processes into efficient, safe, and modern code.

By mastering deep learning with Rust, you are not just learning another programming language—you are stepping into a new paradigm of **reliable, high-performance AI development**.

Part I
Foundations of Deep Learning in Rust

Chapter 1
Introduction

1.1 Introduction

In this chapter, we introduce Rust and explain why it is our choice for deep learning implementation due to its memory safety, concurrency, and performance. We discuss the importance of studying deep learning, highlighting its wide applications, such as image recognition and natural language processing. We provide a road map for studying the book, emphasizing the sequential structure of chapters and the importance of practicing exercises. Supplementary materials, like the GitHub repository, offer access to source code examples and solutions, ensuring the code stays updated with the latest Rust versions. Engaging with these resources will enhance your proficiency in implementing deep learning models in Rust.

1.2 Introduction to Deep Learning and Rust

Artificial intelligence (AI) is transforming industries and everyday life, with deep learning driving much of this change. From applications that predict trends to systems that understand language, AI's rapid advancement has opened up incredible possibilities. But with these advancements comes a critical need for AI systems that are not only high performing but also secure and reliable.

In recent years, breakthroughs in AI have been closely tied to improvements in machine learning techniques, particularly those that can process vast amounts of data. However, creating AI models that are both efficient and safe is a complex challenge. Ensuring that these systems can be implemented and scaled securely is essential, especially as AI technology becomes more integrated into sensitive areas of society and business.

This book introduces the fundamental concepts behind deep learning and explores various types of architectures and their applications. A key aspect we'll cover is implementing these AI models using Rust—a programming language that stands out for its speed, security, and efficiency. Rust is gaining traction in the AI community because it combines principles from several established programming languages, and its design makes it easier for developers to write code that is both performant and memory-safe.

You might wonder why Rust is suited for AI. Known for its robust performance and safe memory management, Rust enables developers to build systems that are both powerful and highly stable. We'll discuss how Rust's unique features, such as concurrency and efficient memory handling, make it an excellent choice for AI applications. Later in this chapter, we'll look at why Rust can outperform other languages in critical ways and how it offers a green, energy-efficient alternative for intensive computing tasks.

The following chapters will dive deeper into the technical details and introduce key concepts, giving you a comprehensive foundation in both AI and Rust's potential for AI development. For now, consider this a starting point—a view of what's possible as we combine the strengths of advanced AI with the stability and efficiency Rust brings to the table.

1.3 Detailed Comparison of Programming Languages

To understand why Rust is an excellent choice for AI and Deep Learning, it's important to compare it in detail with other programming languages. Table 1.1 presents a comparison based on three metrics: energy efficiency, time complexity, and memory usage.

1. **Energy Efficiency**

   - **C (1.00)**: As a low-level language, C is extremely energy efficient, offering fine-grained control over hardware resources.
   - **Rust (1.03)**: Rust's energy efficiency is nearly on par with C, thanks to its ability to perform low-level system operations—such as direct memory management and fine-grained control over hardware resources—while maintaining strong compile-time safety and optimization features.
   - **C++ (1.34)**: While also close to C in terms of efficiency, C++'s additional features can sometimes introduce overhead.
   - **Java (1.95)**: Java's energy consumption is higher due to its virtual machine and garbage collection, which add runtime overhead.
   - **Python (75.88)**: Python, an interpreted language with dynamic typing, is significantly less energy efficient. Its ease of use comes at the cost of higher energy consumption.

Table 1.1 Compare energy efficiency and time complexity of different programming languages [8]

PL	Energy	Time	Mb
C	1.00	1.00	1.17
Rust	1.03	1.04	1.54
C++	1.34	1.56	1.34
Ada	1.70	1.85	1.47
Java	1.95	1.89	6.01
Pascal	2.14	3.02	1.00
Lisp	2.27	3.40	1.92
Ocaml	2.40	3.09	2.82
Fortran	2.52	4.20	1.24
Haskell	3.10	3.55	2.54
C#	3.14	3.14	2.58
Go	3.23	2.83	1.05
F#	4.13	6.30	4.25
JavaScript	4.45	6.52	4.59
Racket	7.91	11.27	3.52
TypeScript	21.50	46.20	4.69
PHP	29.30	27.64	2.57
Ruby	69.91	59.34	3.97
Python	75.88	71.90	2.80
Perl	79.58	65.79	6.62

2. **Time Complexity**

- **C (1.00)**: Known for its speed, C is often used in performance-critical applications.
- **Rust (1.04)**: Rust's performance is comparable to C, making it suitable for high-performance computing.
- **C++ (1.56)**: Offers object-oriented features that can add complexity and slow down execution.
- **Java (1.89)**: Bytecode interpretation and garbage collection can increase execution time.
- **Python (71.90)**: Python's interpreted nature and dynamic typing lead to slower execution times compared to compiled languages.

3. **Memory Usage**

- **C (1.17 MB)**: C is known for its efficient memory usage.
- **Rust (1.54 MB)**: Rust's memory footprint is slightly higher than C's due to its safety model,[1] yet it remains highly efficient.
- **C++ (1.34 MB)**: Similar to C, but object-oriented features can increase memory usage.
- **Java (6.01 MB)**: Higher memory usage due to the JVM and garbage collection.
- **Python (2.80 MB)**: Higher than C and Rust due to its runtime and dynamic typing.

This detailed comparison underscores why Rust is a strong candidate for implementing AI systems. Its balance of energy efficiency, time complexity, and memory usage makes it an optimal choice for high-performance applications where efficiency and speed are crucial.

To illustrate the power of Rust in the context of AI, consider an example where we implement a simple neural network for image classification. In Python, this might involve using libraries such as TensorFlow or PyTorch. While these frameworks are highly optimized at their core—relying on C, C++, and CUDA for the heavy numerical computation—the surrounding Python "glue code" that coordinates these operations can introduce overhead, especially in fine-grained or iterative workloads. Rust, on the other hand, allows developers to build neural networks directly with system-level control, combining high performance with memory safety.

Moreover, Rust's ecosystem includes crates (Rust's term for libraries) like ndarray for numerical computing, autograd for automatic differentiation, linfa for machine learning framework in Rust, providing algorithms and utilities for common machine learning tasks, and tch-rs, which provides bindings for PyTorch, allowing Rust to seamlessly integrate with existing AI tools and frameworks.

1.4 How to Use This Book

This book is not an elementary text on programming, AI, or deep learning. Some prior programming experience is required to follow the material smoothly. While a basic understanding of neural networks is helpful, it is not mandatory. This book is aimed at an intermediate level, so a secondary-school knowledge of mathematics, especially functions, probability, and differential calculus, is crucial for understanding the deep learning concepts introduced here.

Consider this book as a research project. Read each chapter while testing the code and configurations in your preferred operating system. We will provide instructions for installing Rust and its dependencies across various platforms, including Windows, macOS, and Linux, to ensure a smooth start regardless of your setup.

---

[1] While Rust's ownership and borrowing system eliminates many memory errors, its safe abstractions and initialization guarantees can result in marginally higher memory use compared to C's fully manual memory management.

To get the most out of this book, practice the exercises at the end of each chapter before moving on to the next. Some exercises test the coding skills learned in the chapter, while others assess theoretical understanding. These exercises are designed to reinforce concepts and offer hands-on experience with Rust and deep learning.

We also recommend exploring supplementary resources and engaging with the Rust and AI communities. Online forums, GitHub repositories, and Rust's official documentation can provide valuable insights and support as you progress. Active participation in these communities will help you stay updated on the latest developments and best practices in both Rust and deep learning.

The chapters in this book are structured sequentially, with each building on the knowledge introduced in previous ones. While it's designed to be read in order, the structure allows some flexibility, enabling you to skip ahead or revisit certain chapters as needed. This approach ensures that you can navigate through the material in a way that best suits your learning style, while still gaining a cohesive understanding of Rust and deep learning concepts.

1.5   Companion GitHub Repository for Source Code

There is a GitHub repository hosted by Apress that includes the latest version of the code from the book. The repository is updated every six months, with announcements made on the book's website on Apress. The address of the repository is https://github.com/Apress/Deep-Learning-with-Rust?tab=readme-ov-file.

The repository includes the source code for examples explained in the book. By accessing the repository, you can download and run the code on your local machine, enabling you to experiment with the examples and modify them to suit your needs.

Furthermore, the repository provides a platform for collaboration. You can contribute to the repository by suggesting improvements, reporting issues, or even adding new examples and exercises. This collaborative approach enhances the learning experience and fosters a sense of community among readers.

The advantage of a GitHub repository for the book is that the source code will be updated according to the latest version of Rust or its libraries. Also, new developments in functions will be tracked, so you can adjust your code based on recent advancements. This ensures that the book remains relevant and up-to-date, even as the Rust language and its ecosystem continue to evolve.

To summarize, this book aims to equip you with the knowledge and skills necessary to implement Deep Learning algorithms in Rust. By understanding the core principles of Deep Learning and leveraging Rust's unique features, you can build efficient, secure, and high-performance AI systems. As you progress through the chapters, you will gain a deeper appreciation for the interplay between theory and practice, ultimately becoming proficient in both Deep Learning and Rust.

Problems

1.1 List and explain at least three features of Rust that make it suitable for deep learning applications.

1.2 Compare Rust's memory management with that of Java, focusing on the absence of garbage collection in Rust.

1.3 Illustrate how Rust's concurrency model can prevent data race in AI applications.

Chapter 2
Introduction to Deep Learning in Rust

2.1 Introduction

This chapter aims to establish a solid foundation in deep learning, highlight Rust's unique advantages for AI development, and ensure your development environment is fully set up for building high-performance AI applications. By the end, you'll have a clearer understanding of why Rust is an excellent choice for AI, particularly deep learning, and be equipped with the tools and libraries necessary to start coding.

2.2 Overview of Deep Learning

Deep learning represents a powerful branch of machine learning that leverages complex neural networks to learn and make decisions based on large volumes of data. Unlike traditional algorithms that require manual feature engineering, deep learning models can automatically learn representations from raw data, making them especially effective for complex tasks such as image recognition, language translation, and even game playing. This section introduces deep learning by covering its foundational concepts, its impact across various industries, and why its computational demands make language choice critical.

2.2.1 Foundational Concepts in Deep Learning

At the core of deep learning are neural networks, computational models inspired by the human brain's structure. These networks consist of layers of nodes (often called neurons) connected by weighted edges, with each layer transforming input data to uncover intricate patterns. The deeper the network—meaning the more layers it has—the more complex relationships it can model, enabling tasks like recognizing objects in images or translating languages.

A few essential components define neural networks:

- **Layers**: Neural networks are structured in layers—input, hidden, and output layers, Figure 2.1. Each hidden layer allows the network to learn progressively complex patterns, enabling it to extract high-level features from raw data.

© Mehrdad Maleki 2026
M. Maleki, *Deep Learning with Rust*, https://doi.org/10.1007/979-8-8688-2208-7_2

Figure 2.1 Feed-forward
neural network

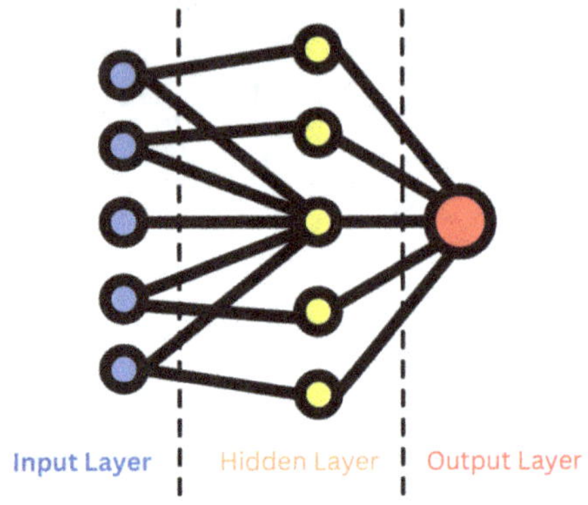

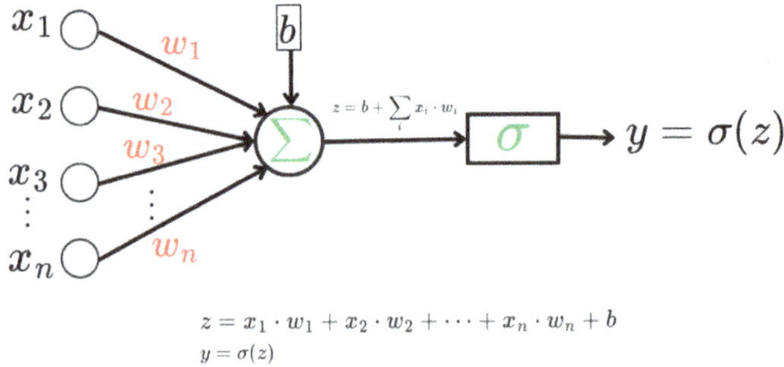

$$z = x_1 \cdot w_1 + x_2 \cdot w_2 + \cdots + x_n \cdot w_n + b$$
$$y = \sigma(z)$$

Figure 2.2 Perceptron

The basic building block of a neural network is the perceptron. A perceptron takes several input values and produces a single output. Each input is associated with a weight, which represents how strongly that input influences the output. In addition, the perceptron has a bias, a constant term that allows the model to shift the output of the activation function independently of the input values, Figure 2.2. Mathematically, the perceptron first computes a weighted sum of its inputs and adds the bias term. This linear combination forms the perceptron's raw output before any nonlinearity is applied.

Next, this raw value passes through an activation function, which is a nonlinear transformation such as the sigmoid, ReLU (Rectified Linear Unit), or tanh function. The activation function determines whether a neuron "fires" and introduces nonlinearity into the model, enabling the network to represent complex, nonlinear relationships between inputs and outputs. Without this nonlinearity, the network would be equivalent to a single linear transformation, regardless of its depth.

Training a perceptron involves adjusting its weights and bias so that its predicted output matches the desired output as closely as possible. This adjustment process is driven by learning from data—a collection of input-output pairs known as the training dataset. Initially, the weights are set randomly. The perceptron computes predictions for each input, and the difference between the predicted and actual outputs (the error) is measured. Using a learning algorithm such as backpropagation, this error is propagated backward through the network to update the weights. The updates are performed iteratively, gradually reducing the error until the model reaches a state where further changes to the weights produce minimal improvement. Once trained, the perceptron can generalize from its training data and predict outputs for new, unseen inputs drawn from the same underlying distribution.

- **Activation Functions**: Activation functions introduce nonlinearity into the network, allowing it to model complex patterns. Functions like ReLU (Rectified Linear Unit) and sigmoid are commonly

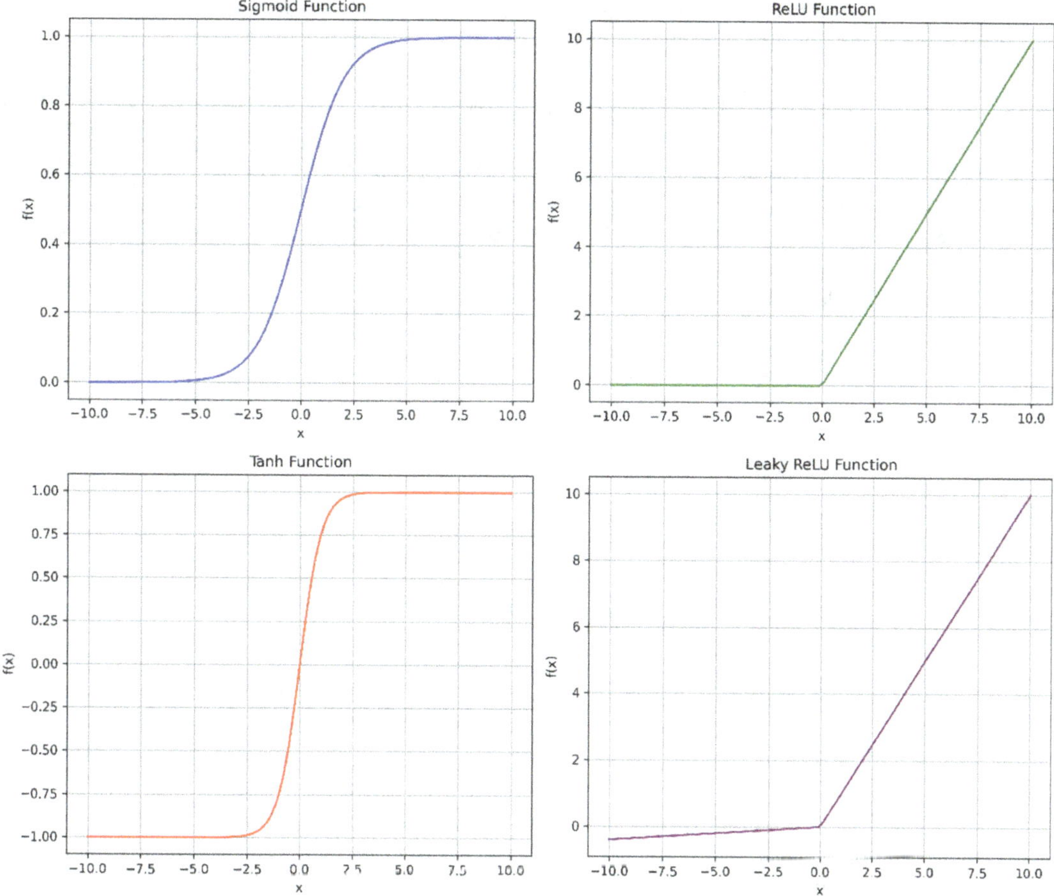

Figure 2.3 Activation functions

used to activate neurons, determining whether each neuron should "fire" based on the input it receives.

Several commonly used activation functions include (Figure 2.3):

1. **Sigmoid:** The range of the sigmoid is between 0 and 1. This function is differentiable everywhere and tends toward 1 for large positive input values and 0 for large negative input values. The formula of the sigmoid is as follows:

$$\sigma(x) = \frac{1}{1 + e^{-x}}$$

   Since the values of the sigmoid function are between 0 and 1, it can be interpreted as a probability distribution, making it suitable for binary classification. Specifically, the predicted label is 1 if the value of the sigmoid is greater than or equal to 0.5, and the predicted label is 0 if the value of the sigmoid function is less than 0.5. The main drawback of the sigmoid function is the "vanishing gradient" problem, which we will explain later, as it can negatively affect the learning process.

2. **ReLU (Rectified Linear Unit):** The ReLU function is one of the most popular activation functions. This function returns zero for negative input values and acts as the identity function

for positive input values, i.e., it returns the input as the output for positive values. This function represents sparsity. The formula of ReLU is as follows:

$$\mathrm{ReLU}(x) = max(0, x)$$

The problem with ReLU is that it suffers from the "dying ReLU" issue: if all the inputs are negative, ReLU never activates. To address this challenge, Leaky ReLU has been proposed.

3. **Leaky ReLU:** As mentioned in the ReLU function section, Leaky ReLU has been proposed to address the issue of "dying ReLU" by introducing a very small gradient for negative values. The formula of Leaky ReLU is as follows:

$$\mathrm{Leaky\ ReLU}(x) = \begin{cases} x & \text{if } x > 0 \\ \alpha x & \text{if } x \leq 0 \end{cases}$$

where α is a very small positive number.

4. **Tanh:** The tanh, which stands for hyperbolic tangent, is similar to the sigmoid function, but with one difference: the range of tanh is between -1 and 1. The formula of tanh is as follows:

$$\tanh(x) = \frac{e^x - e^{-x}}{e^x + e^{-x}}$$

This function is differentiable everywhere and, like the sigmoid, suffers from the "vanishing gradient" problem. Due to its symmetry around the center of the coordinate system, it can model more complex patterns than the sigmoid. It is commonly used in Recurrent Neural Networks (RNNs).

5. **Softmax:** It is used in multi-class classification problems. The input to this function is a real-valued score, which is then converted into a probability distribution. If there are n classes, the softmax function predicts the probability of belonging to each of these classes. Therefore, the sum of all softmax values should be equal to 1. The formula of the softmax is as follows:

$$\mathrm{softmax}(x_i) = \frac{e^{x_i}}{\sum_j e^{x_j}}$$

- **Loss Functions and Optimization**: A **loss function** measures how far the network's predictions are from the actual target values. It provides a quantitative measure of the model's error during training. The goal of training is to find the set of weights **w** and biases **b** that minimize this loss across all training examples.

  If the network produces a prediction $\hat{y}$ for a true output y, the loss function $L(y, \hat{y})$ expresses the difference between them. For example, in regression problems, a common choice is the **Mean Squared Error (MSE)**:

$$L(y, \hat{y}) = \frac{1}{2}(y - \hat{y})^2 \tag{2.1}$$

  In classification problems, a more appropriate choice is the **Cross-Entropy Loss**, which measures the distance between two probability distributions—the true label distribution y and the predicted probability distribution $\hat{y}$:

$$L(y, \hat{y}) = -\sum_{i=1}^{C} y_i \log(\hat{y}_i) \tag{2.2}$$

Here, C is the number of classes, and y_i equals 1 if the sample belongs to class i, and 0 otherwise.

An **optimization algorithm** iteratively updates the model parameters (weights and biases) to minimize the loss function. The most widely used optimization method is **gradient descent**. In gradient descent, each parameter is updated in the opposite direction of the gradient of the loss with respect to that parameter.

Differentiation

The derivative of a function $f : \mathbb{R} \to \mathbb{R}$ calculates the rate of change of the output with respect to small changes in the input. Mathematically, the derivative of the function f at x, denoted as $f'(x)$, is defined by the following limit:

$$f'(x) = \lim_{h \to 0} \frac{f(x + h) - f(x)}{h}$$

If we assume $y = f(x)$, then other notations for the derivative of f at x are $\frac{dy}{dx}$ or $\frac{df}{dx}$.
If $f : \mathbb{R}^n \to \mathbb{R}$ is a multivariable function, the concept of the derivative differs from that of a single-variable function. Since this function has multiple inputs and just one output, we need to consider the rate of change of the output with respect to each input. For example, if $y = f(x_1, \cdots, x_n)$, then the rate of change of the output with respect to the ith input is denoted by $\frac{\partial y}{\partial x_i}$ or $\frac{\partial f}{\partial x_i}$, which is called **partial derivative** of f with respect to the x_i, and is defined similarly to the derivative of a single-valued function, i.e.:

$$\frac{\partial y}{\partial x_i} = \lim_{h \to 0} \frac{f(x_1, \cdots, x_i + h, \cdots, x_n) - f(x_1, \cdots, x_i, \cdots, x_n)}{h}$$

The gradient of the function $f : \mathbb{R}^n \to \mathbb{R}$ at the input $\mathbf{x} = (x_1, \cdots, x_n)$ is a vector of dimension n, where each element of this vector is the partial derivative of the output with respect to each input, i.e.:

$$\nabla f(\mathbf{x}) = \left(\frac{\partial f}{\partial x_1}, \cdots, \frac{\partial f}{\partial x_n} \right)$$

The gradient $\nabla f(\mathbf{x})$ of a function $f(\mathbf{x})$ points in the direction of the steepest *increase*, while the negative gradient $- \nabla f(\mathbf{x})$ points toward the steepest *decrease*.
The "rate of change" here is a *signed quantity*, expressed by the **directional derivative**:

$$D_{\mathbf{v}} f(\mathbf{x}) = \nabla f(\mathbf{x}) \cdot \mathbf{v} \tag{2.3}$$

If the angle between ∇f and $\mathbf{v}$ is acute, the dot product is positive and f increases in that direction; if the angle is obtuse, it is negative and f decreases. The sign thus indicates direction of change, while the magnitude reflects how fast f changes along $\mathbf{v}$.

Gradient Descent

To find the minimum value of a function, we can use properties of the gradient. Suppose $f : \mathbb{R}^n \to \mathbb{R}$ is the function whose minimum value we seek. Let's start with a guess for the minimum value, say $\mathbf{x_0}$. If we move in the opposite direction of the gradient of f at $\mathbf{x_0}$, we arrive at a new point with a smaller f value (Figure 2.4). We repeat this process until the changes become minimal.

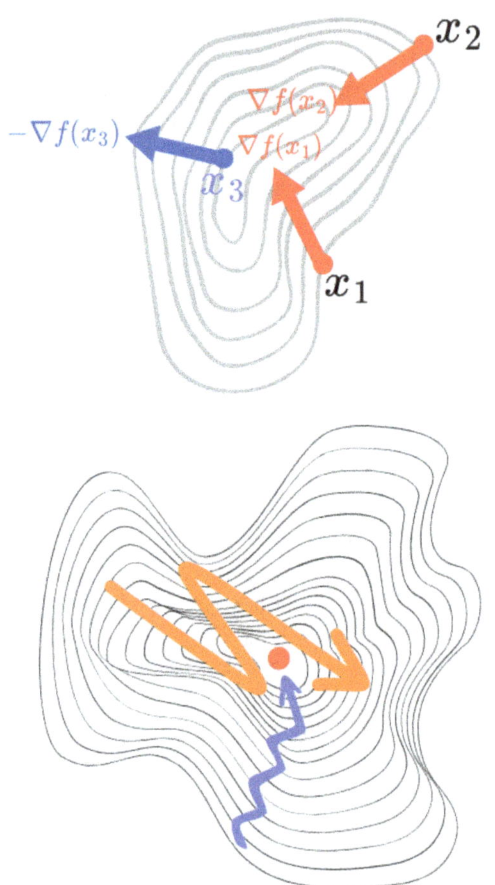

Figure 2.4 The contour of a function $f : \mathbb{R}^2 \to \mathbb{R}$ showing the gradient vectors at different points. As illustrated, at points x_1 and x_2, the movement is directed toward the peak (following the direction of the gradient), while at x_3, located at the peak, the movement is in the opposite direction of the gradient

Figure 2.5 Comparison of two scenarios for the learning rate. The small learning rate (blue path) reaches the minimum but does so slowly. In contrast, the large learning rate (orange path) overshoots the minimum and causes divergence

1. Start with a guess $\mathbf{x_0}$.
2. Update using $\mathbf{x_{t+1}} = \mathbf{x_t} - \alpha \nabla f(\mathbf{x_t})$.
3. If $\|\mathbf{x_{t+1}} - \mathbf{x_t}\| \leq \epsilon$, where $\epsilon > 0$ is a very small error bound, then stop; otherwise, go to step 2.

Here, α is the **learning rate**, which determines the length of each update step. It is a hyperparameter that must be tuned carefully: if α is too large, the algorithm may overshoot the minimum; if it is too small, convergence becomes slow.

In basic gradient descent, α is kept constant for simplicity and stability, but in practice, many optimization algorithms use a *variable learning rate* that adapts over time (e.g., learning rate schedules or adaptive methods such as Adam and RMSProp (Root Mean Square Propagation)) to improve convergence.

The loss function measures the deviation of the neural network's predicted value from the actual data. Suppose the output of the neural network for input $\mathbf{x} = (x_1, \cdots, x_n)$ is $\hat{y}$ and the weights of the neural network are $\boldsymbol{\theta}$. The loss function is thus a function of the weights and inputs. However, since the inputs and outputs are predetermined, the only variables are the weights, i.e.:

$$\mathcal{L} = \mathcal{L}(\boldsymbol{\theta})$$

Let $NN(\mathbf{x}; \boldsymbol{\theta}) = \hat{y}$ represent the neural network's prediction for input $\mathbf{x}$ and weights $\boldsymbol{\theta}$. To adjust the weights and minimize the loss function, we apply gradient descent on the loss function with respect to the weights.

Algorithm 2.1 Gradient descent for neural network training

Require: Training data $\{(x^{(i)}, y^{(i)})\}$ for $i = 1, \ldots, m$
Require: Learning rate α
Require: Loss function $\mathcal{L}$
Require: Initial weights and biases θ (randomly initialized)
Ensure: Optimized weights and biases θ
 1: Initialize θ (weights and biases) with small random values.
 2: **while** not converged **do**
 3:    **for** each training example $(x^{(i)}, y^{(i)})$ **do**
 4:       **Feedforward Pass:**
        Compute the network's output $\hat{y}^{(i)} = NN(x^{(i)}; \theta)$ using the current parameters θ.
 5:       **Compute Loss:**
        Calculate the loss for the current example:
        $\mathcal{L}^{(i)} = \mathcal{L}(\hat{y}^{(i)}, y^{(i)})$
 6:       **Backpropagation:**
        Compute the gradient of the loss with respect to each parameter in θ:
        $\nabla_{\theta} \mathcal{L}^{(i)}$
 7:       **Gradient Descent Update:**
        Update each parameter in θ using the learning rate α:
        $\theta = \theta - \alpha \cdot \nabla_{\theta} \mathcal{L}^{(i)}$
 8:    **end for**
 9:    Check for convergence:
       If $\|\theta_{\text{new}} - \theta_{\text{old}}\| < \epsilon$ (where ϵ is a small threshold), then stop.
10: **end while**
11: **return** Optimized parameters θ.

One of the most important elements in designing a robust neural network is choosing an appropriate loss function based on the nature of the problem. Here is a list of the most important loss functions, depending on specific problem types:

1. **Mean Squared Error (MSE):** This loss function measures the mean value of squared differences between all pairs of predicted and actual values. It is a differentiable function and is used for regression problems. It penalizes large errors. The formula for MSE is as follows:

$$\text{MSE} = \frac{1}{N} \sum_{i=1}^{N} (\hat{y}_i - y_i)^2$$

2. **Mean Absolute Error (MAE):** This is similar to MSE but uses the absolute value of the difference rather than the square of the difference. It is not differentiable and is less sensitive to outliers. The formula for MAE is as follows:

$$\text{MAE} = \frac{1}{N} \sum_{i=1}^{N} |\hat{y}_i - y_i|$$

3. **Cross-Entropy Loss (Log Loss):** This loss function is used in classification problems.

(a) For binary classification, where labels are binary (0/1), the label of the i-th dataset is y_i, a binary variable. The output of the neural network, $\hat{y}_i$, is the predicted probability (a real number between 0 and 1). The formula for binary classification is as follows:

$$\text{Cross-Entropy} = -\frac{1}{N} \sum_{i=1}^{N} \left(y_i \log \hat{y}_i + (1 - y_i) \log(1 - \hat{y}_i) \right)$$

(b) For multi-class classification, assuming that the total number of classes, C, is greater than 2, the formula for the loss function is as follows:

$$\text{Cross-Entropy} = -\frac{1}{N} \sum_{i=1}^{N} \sum_{c \in C} y_{i,c} \log \hat{y}_{i,c}$$

where $y_{i,c}$ is the true label for class c and $\hat{y}_{i,c}$ is the predicted probability of belonging to class c.

4. **Kullback-Leibler Divergence (KL Divergence):** This measures the difference between two probability distributions. Its application is in variational autoencoders (VAEs), which are generative models with a prior and noise distribution. The KL Divergence of probability distributions P and Q is defined as follows:

$$KL(P\|Q) = \sum_{i} P(i) \log \frac{P(i)}{Q(i)}$$

5. **Cosine Similarity Loss:** Commonly used to measure the similarity between two vectors—such as sentence embeddings in NLP or user–item representations in recommendation systems. It computes the cosine of the angle between the predicted and actual vectors, yielding a value in the interval $[-1, 1]$. A value of -1 indicates exact opposition, $+1$ indicates perfect similarity, and 0 denotes no correlation. The formula is given by:

$$\text{Cosine Similarity} = \frac{\sum_i y_i \hat{y}_i}{\|y\| \, \|\hat{y}\|}$$

The core of the learning process is the **backpropagation** algorithm. We won't go into the details of backpropagation in this book, but it is important to know that in the gradient descent algorithm, we need to calculate the derivative of the loss function with respect to each weight. This process starts from the final layer and recursively computes the derivative of the loss function with respect to each layer.

There are libraries like TensorFlow and PyTorch that compute backpropagation automatically using automatic differentiation. We will show you how to implement gradient descent using similar tools in Rust.

2.2.2 Applications of Deep Learning

Deep Learning has various applications across different types of problems and industries. Of course, Deep Learning is a dynamic field, and new applications emerge every day. Here, we list some notable applications of deep learning.

2.2.2.1 Healthcare

Healthcare is entering a new era where abundant biomedical data play a critical role. Precision medicine, for instance, seeks to tailor treatments to individual patients by integrating data such as molecular traits, environment, electronic health records (EHRs), and lifestyle.

While these data provide great opportunities for machine learning-based medical tools, challenges like high dimensionality, heterogeneity, temporal dependency, and inconsistency hinder their full potential. Harmonizing conflicting medical ontologies (e.g., SNOMED-CT, UMLS, ICD-9) and resolving variations in how clinical phenotypes are expressed, such as identifying "type 2 diabetes mellitus" through diverse data points, remain significant hurdles. Overcoming these barriers is essential to advance reliable, data-driven medical solutions [7].

2.2.2.2 Finance and Bank

Deep learning and AI have transformed finance and banking by automating processes, enhancing decision-making, and ensuring compliance. From retail and commercial lending operations to customer service, AI applications are reducing manual effort, minimizing errors, and accelerating workflows. For example, AI can evaluate credit applications using predictive models, automate document processing for loans, and provide personalized credit scoring.

In investments, robo-advisors offer tailored portfolio management based on customer preferences and risk appetite. AI also optimizes operational tasks like debt collection, invoice automation, and account reconciliation, improving efficiency and reducing costs. In insurance, AI assists in pricing, claims processing, and fraud detection, while audit and compliance tasks benefit from scalable AI systems that analyze regulations and identify noncompliance.

AI further enhances customer service through chatbots and by identifying upsell opportunities or preventing customer churn with predictive modeling. Additionally, AI-driven trading systems analyze market patterns for better investment decisions. These applications collectively showcase AI's role in making finance faster, smarter, and more secure [2].

2.2.2.3 Natural Language Processing (NLP)

Deep learning has revolutionized NLP, enabling machines to comprehend, interpret, and generate human language with remarkable precision. It excels in tasks like sentiment analysis, machine translation, text summarization, and chatbot development, using neural networks to capture the complexities and nuances of language.

Traditional rule-based systems and statistical methods have been replaced by deep learning models that learn hierarchical representations of text data. These models process vast datasets, extracting both local and global dependencies, and perform tasks like named entity recognition and question answering with unprecedented accuracy.

Key advancements, such as transformer-based architectures (e.g., BERT, GPT), have significantly enhanced machine translation and contextual understanding by leveraging attention mechanisms to capture long-range dependencies in text. The ability to handle massive datasets and adapt to specific tasks through fine-tuning makes deep learning a powerful tool for creating efficient and robust NLP applications.

In summary, deep learning continues to drive innovation in NLP, bridging the gap between human language and machine understanding across diverse fields like healthcare, customer service, and beyond [1].

2.2.2.4 Generative Applications

Generative models have transformed the way machines create content, with Generative Adversarial Networks (GANs) being among the earliest breakthroughs [3]. Introduced as a pioneering framework,

GANs consist of two networks—a generator and a discriminator—working in tandem to produce realistic images, videos, and other content. This approach laid the foundation for generative tasks like image synthesis and deepfake creation, where GANs excel in mimicking real-world data.

Building on these foundations, advanced models like GPT (Generative Pre-trained Transformer) series have taken generative applications to new heights, especially in text generation. Leveraging transformer-based architectures and pre-training on massive corpora, GPT models can generate human-like text, craft coherent stories, answer questions, and even assist in creative tasks like coding and poetry. These advancements demonstrate the growing potential of generative models across domains, including visual media, text synthesis, and beyond.

The versatility of deep learning has fueled its integration into numerous other areas, including retail, manufacturing, and entertainment. It's precisely this broad applicability and potential for high impact that has spurred interest in programming languages capable of efficiently supporting deep learning workflows.

2.2.3 Why Language Choice Matters in Deep Learning

Deep learning demands significant computational power and efficient use of resources, particularly when working with large datasets or complex models. Thus, the choice of programming language plays a critical role in the performance, scalability, and reliability of deep learning applications.

Historically, deep learning research has leaned heavily on languages like Python, largely due to its extensive library ecosystem (TensorFlow, PyTorch, etc.) and ease of use. However, Python's limitations in performance and memory efficiency have led developers to explore languages like Rust for specific applications. Rust offers low-level memory control, high performance, and strong concurrency support—qualities that make it well suited to meet the demands of modern deep learning.

In summary, deep learning combines powerful neural networks, vast data processing, and complex computations to solve advanced problems across industries. As the demands on these models grow, so does the need for efficient, high-performance programming languages like Rust, which we'll explore in detail in the next section. Here, we'll look at Rust's potential to tackle the unique challenges of deep learning, providing a compelling alternative for those interested in scalable and high-performance AI applications.

2.3 The Rust Advantage in AI Development

Rust brings a unique set of advantages to the table, making it an ideal language for developing AI applications that require both performance and reliability. Here, we'll explore how Rust's core strengths align with the demands of AI and deep learning:

Performance: Rust's close-to-the-metal execution is often compared to C and C++, making it suitable for applications where speed is crucial. Its design allows for low-level memory management, resulting in efficient, predictable performance.

Safety: Rust's strict compile-time checks, ownership model, and borrow checker ensure **memory safety**—preventing issues such as dangling pointers, null pointer dereferencing, and data races. While Rust's ownership rules also help minimize memory leaks by automatically freeing most unused resources, safe Rust can still leak memory intentionally or through reference cycles. These safety guarantees are especially valuable in AI applications, where data integrity and reproducibility are critical.

Concurrency: Rust's concurrency model is designed to handle multi-threading safely, which is essential in deep learning for handling large datasets and parallel computation tasks. By avoiding data races, Rust ensures stable and secure multi-threading, making it well suited for AI applications that involve concurrent processing.

In this section, we'll discuss how these advantages translate to more efficient, safer, and scalable AI systems. Additionally, we'll touch on the growing ecosystem of Rust libraries for machine learning and scientific computing, which makes Rust an increasingly viable option for AI research and development.

2.4   Setting Up Your Rust Environment for AI

With a solid understanding of Rust's advantages, we're now ready to set up a development environment that leverages Rust's power for AI applications. This section will guide you through:

1. Installing Rust

   - Detailed steps for installing Rust on various platforms (Windows, macOS, and Linux).
   - Tips on using rustup, Rust's version manager, to ensure you're working with the latest stable version.

2. Installing Essential Libraries (Crates)

   - **Numerical Computing**: The ndarray crate offers N-dimensional array support, similar to NumPy in Python, and is essential for handling data in Rust.
   - **Machine Learning Frameworks**: We'll introduce crates like linfa, which offers a suite of machine learning algorithms, and tch-rs, which provides bindings to PyTorch, allowing Rust to integrate seamlessly with existing Python-based AI workflows.
   - **Automatic Differentiation**: The autograd crate is available for creating differentiable programs, which is key in training deep neural networks.

3. Optimizing Rust for AI Workflows

   - **Toolchain Configuration**: Recommendations for optimizing Rust's toolchain for AI development, including performance flags and debugging options.
   - **Managing Dependencies and Crate Versions**: Guidance on maintaining up-to-date libraries while ensuring compatibility, especially for projects involving large-scale data processing and model training.

Through these setup steps, you'll be fully equipped to dive into Rust-based AI development. With a configured environment and key libraries installed, you'll be ready to experiment with Rust's unique features in real-world AI projects.

2.4.1   Installing Rust

In this section, we will guide you through the process of installing Rust on different operating systems, including Linux, macOS, and Windows.

2.4.1.1 Linux and macOS

Before we proceed, it is essential to ensure your system meets the prerequisites and is up-to-date.

Update Your System (Linux)
For Linux users, it is recommended to update your system to avoid compatibility issues. Run the following command in your terminal:

```bash
$ sudo apt update && sudo apt upgrade -y
```

Install Xcode Command-Line Tools (macOS)
For macOS users, Rust requires build tools to compile programs. These tools can be installed by running the following command in your terminal:

```bash
$ xcode-select --install
```

The Common Steps for Linux and macOS
After preparing your system, the installation process for Rust is identical for Linux and macOS.

Download and Run the Rust Installation Script
Use the official Rust installation script, "rustup," to install Rust. Run the following command:

```bash
$ curl --proto '=https' --tlsv1.2 -sSf https://sh.rustup.rs | sh
```

The installation script will guide you through the process. By default, it installs the stable version of Rust.

Add Rust to Your PATH
Once the installation is complete, add Rust to your shell's environment by sourcing the updated profile:

```bash
$ source $HOME/.cargo/env
```

2.4.1.2   Windows

For Windows users, the installation process is slightly different. Follow these steps:

Download and Install Rust
Visit the official Rust website at https://www.rust-lang.org/tools/install and follow the provided instructions. During the installation process, you will be prompted to install Visual Studio, which provides the linker and native libraries necessary to compile programs.

If you require additional guidance during this step, refer to the official documentation: https://rust-lang.github.io/rustup/installation/windows-msvc.html.

Command Compatibility
The rest of this book will use commands compatible with both "cmd.exe" and PowerShell. If there are specific differences in commands, they will be explicitly mentioned.

Rust installation is now complete across all major operating systems. You can proceed with your development environment fully configured!

2.4.2   Tips for Using `rustup`

The `rustup` tool is Rust's official version manager, making it easy to install, update, and manage different versions of Rust. Below are some tips to ensure you're always working with the latest stable version and managing Rust efficiently.

2.4.2.1   Update to the Latest Stable Version

Keep your Rust installation up-to-date by running the following command:

```bash
$ rustup update
```

This command updates all installed toolchains (e.g., stable, beta, nightly) to their latest versions. After updating, ensure you are using the stable version by running:

```bash
$ rustup default stable
```

2.4.2.2   Switch Between Versions

If your project requires a specific version of Rust, you can install and switch to it using:

bash

```bash
$ rustup install <version>
$ rustup default <version>
```

Example
To install and set version 1.70.0 as the default:

bash

```bash
$ rustup install 1.70.0
$ rustup default 1.70.0
```

2.4.2.3 Override Rust Version for a Project

To use a specific Rust version in a particular project directory, set an override with:

bash

```bash
$ rustup override set <version>
```

Example
To use the nightly version in a project:

bash

```bash
$ rustup override set nightly
```

This ensures the specified version is used whenever you're in that directory.

2.4.2.4 Remove Unnecessary Versions

Over time, older Rust versions may accumulate. To free up space, remove unused versions with:

bash

```bash
$ rustup uninstall <version>
```

Example
To remove version 1.65.0:

```bash
$ rustup uninstall 1.65.0
```

2.4.2.5   Explore Installed Components

To view the installed versions and components, use:

```bash
$ rustup show
```

This command displays the default toolchain, active overrides, and the current Rust version in use.

2.4.2.6   Use Nightly or Beta Channels

For experimenting with the latest features, you can install and switch to the nightly or beta channels:

```bash
$ rustup install nightly
$ rustup default nightly
```

Note: Nightly or beta channels may not be as stable as the stable release, so use them cautiously.

2.4.3   Cargo: Rust's Package Manager

Cargo is Rust's powerful package manager and build system. It simplifies managing dependencies, compiling projects, and running tests, making it an essential tool for Rust development. With Cargo, developers can efficiently handle the complexities of modern software development, especially in AI workflows where dependencies and version management are critical.

Installing and Using Cargo
Cargo is installed by default when you install Rust using `rustup`. You can verify its installation by running:

```bash
$ cargo --version
```

This command outputs the installed version of Cargo, confirming its availability.

Key Features of Cargo
- **Creating Projects:** Cargo can initialize a new Rust project with all the necessary files and directories.
- **Dependency Management:** Automatically downloads, updates, and manages external libraries (crates).
- **Building Projects:** Compiles Rust code and ensures all dependencies are included.
- **Testing and Benchmarking:** Provides built-in support for writing and running tests.

Example: Creating a New Project
You can create a new Rust project using the `cargo new` command:

```bash
$ cargo new my_project
```

```
1    Created binary (application) `new_project` package
```

This command creates a directory named `my_project` with the following structure:

```
1  my_project/
2  |- Cargo.toml
3  |- src/
4      |- main.rs
```

The `Cargo.toml` file contains metadata about the project and its dependencies, while `src/main.rs` contains the entry point of the Rust application.

Building and Running a Project
Navigate to the project directory and use Cargo to build and run the project:

```bash
$ cd my_project
$ cargo build
$ cargo run
```

The `cargo build` command compiles the project, and `cargo run` builds and executes it.

Accessing Rust Documentation
Cargo makes accessing Rust's offline documentation straightforward. Run the following command:

```bash
$ rustup doc
```

This opens the Rust documentation in your default web browser, providing access to comprehensive resources, including the standard library and Cargo's features.

Testing with Cargo
Cargo also includes tools for running tests:

```bash
$ cargo test
```

This command automatically discovers and executes all tests in the project, ensuring that your code is functioning as expected.

Cargo is an integral part of Rust's ecosystem, streamlining project management, dependency handling, and documentation access. Its versatility and efficiency make it a powerful tool for developers, especially in the complex environments of AI development. By leveraging Cargo, you can focus on building robust applications without worrying about the intricacies of managing dependencies and build systems.

2.4.3.1   Revert to a Clean State

If you encounter issues or wish to start fresh, you can uninstall and reinstall Rust using:

```bash
$ rustup self uninstall
```

DON'T RUN THIS CODE.

2.4.3.2   Best Practices

- Regularly update your toolchains with `rustup update` to benefit from the latest features and security patches.
- Use overrides for projects that require specific Rust versions to maintain compatibility.
- Keep your environment clean by uninstalling unused versions of Rust.

By following these tips, you can effectively manage Rust versions and ensure you're always using the optimal toolchain for your projects.

2.4.4   Installing Essential Libraries (Crates)

Rust's ecosystem includes several powerful libraries, known as crates, that are essential for numerical computing, machine learning, and automatic differentiation. These crates enable developers to implement complex AI algorithms efficiently in Rust. Below, we outline the key crates, their features, and how to install and verify them.

2.4.4.1   Numerical Computing: `ndarray`

The `ndarray` crate provides support for N-dimensional arrays, similar to NumPy in Python. It is essential for data manipulation and numerical computations in Rust.

Installation
Install the `ndarray` crate by adding it to your project's dependencies in the `Cargo.toml` file:

```bash
$ cargo add ndarray
```

Alternatively, you can manually add the following line to the `Cargo.toml` file:

2.4.4.2   Manually Adding Dependencies to `Cargo.toml`

To manually add a dependency to the `Cargo.toml` file, follow these steps:

1. Locate the `Cargo.toml` File

Navigate to the root directory of your Rust project. The `Cargo.toml` file is located here. If it doesn't exist, initialize a new project using:

```bash
$ cargo init
```

2. Open the `Cargo.toml` File

Open the `Cargo.toml` file in your preferred text editor, such as `vim`, `nano`, or a graphical editor like VS Code.

3. Add the Dependency

Inside the [dependencies] section of the file, manually add the crate name and its version. For example, to add the `ndarray` crate:

```
[dependencies]
ndarray = "0.15"
```

If the [dependencies] section does not exist, create it at the bottom of the file.

4. Save the Changes

Save the file and close the editor after adding the dependency.

5. Update the Dependencies

Run the following command to download and compile the dependency:

```bash
$ cargo build
```

This will ensure that Cargo fetches the crate from the Rust package registry (`crates.io`) and adds it to your project.

Example of a `Cargo.toml` File

Here's an example of a typical `Cargo.toml` file with the `ndarray` crate added:

```
[package]
name = ''my_project''
version = "0.1.0"
edition = "2021"

[dependencies]
ndarray = "0.15"
```

6. Verification

To verify that the dependency works, use it in your Rust program. For example:

```rust
use ndarray::Array;

fn main() {
    let arr = Array::from_vec(vec![1, 2, 3]);
    println!("Array: {:?}", arr);
}
```

Run the program using:

```bash
$ cargo run
```

If the output displays the array, the dependency has been successfully added and is functioning correctly. This should be the output:

```
Array: [1, 2, 3], shape=[3], strides=[1], layout=CFcf (0xf),
    const ndim=1
```

2.4.4.3   Machine Learning Frameworks

Rust offers several machine learning crates that facilitate the development of AI models:

linfa: A Machine Learning Framework
The linfa crate provides a suite of machine learning algorithms, including classification, regression, and clustering.

Installation
Add linfa to your project:

```bash
$ cargo add linfa
```

2.4.5   *Installing and Testing Linfa*

Add the following dependency to your `Cargo.toml` file:

```
[dependencies]
linfa = "0.4"
ndarray = "0.15"
```

Note that Linfa depends on specific versions of the `ndarray` crate. As of this writing, `linfa = "0.4"` is compatible with `ndarray = "0.15"`. Newer versions of `ndarray` may introduce API changes that prevent Linfa from compiling. If you encounter compilation errors related to `ndarray` traits or macros (such as `array!`), downgrade `ndarray` to version `0.15`.

You can verify your installation with the following example:

```rust
use linfa::Dataset;
use ndarray::array;

fn main() {
    let features = array![[1.0, 2.0], [3.0, 4.0]];
    let targets = array![0, 1];
    let dataset = Dataset::new(features, targets);
    println!("Linfa dataset: {:?}", dataset);
}
```

If this example fails to compile, check the `Cargo.lock` file to confirm that `ndarray = "0.15"` is being used.

The output is as follows:

```
Linfa dataset: DatasetBase { records: [[1.0, 2.0],[3.0, 4.0]],
shape=[2, 2], strides=[2, 1], layout=Cc (0x5), const ndim=2,
 targets: [0, 1], shape=[2], strides=[1], layout=CFcf (0xf),
 const ndim=1, weights: [], shape=[0], strides=[0],
 layout=CFcf (0xf), const ndim=1, feature_names: [] }
```

This test confirms that:

1. The linfa crate has been successfully added to your project.
2. The crate can be imported and used without issues.

If you encounter any errors, ensure the crate version in Cargo.toml matches the latest version available and re-run the commands to build your project.

tch-rs: PyTorch Bindings for Rust

The `tch-rs` crate provides bindings to PyTorch, enabling Rust developers to leverage PyTorch's features within Rust projects.

Installation

Install `tch-rs` by adding it to your project:

bash

```bash
$ cargo add tch
```

Additionally, ensure you have PyTorch installed on your system. Refer to the PyTorch installation guide for platform-specific instructions: https://pytorch.org/. Refer to the official https://github.com/LaurentMazare/tch-rs repository for detailed installation instructions and troubleshooting.

Verification

Run a simple PyTorch tensor operation using `tch-rs`:

```rust
use tch::Tensor;

fn main() {
    // Use f_from_slice to create a Tensor
    let tensor = Tensor::f_from_slice(&[1, 2, 3]).expect("
        Failed to create tensor");
    println!("Tensor: {:?}", tensor);
}
```

Compile and run the program:

bash

```bash
$ cargo run
```

Expected Output

When running the provided Rust code using the `tch-rs` crate, the output should display the PyTorch tensor created from the array `[1, 2, 3]`. The expected output is:

```
Tensor: [1, 2, 3]
```

Explanation of the Output

- **Tensor: [1, 2, 3]**: This shows the data contained within the tensor, which corresponds to the input slice `&[1, 2, 3]`.

Confirmation of Successful Installation

If this output appears, it confirms that:

- The `tch-rs` crate is correctly installed and functional.
- PyTorch is successfully integrated with the Rust environment through `tch-rs`.

2.4.5.1 Automatic Differentiation: `autograd`

The `autograd` crate automates the computation of gradients, a critical component for training deep neural networks.

Installation

Add `autograd` to your project:

```bash
$ cargo add autograd
```

Alternatively, edit the `Cargo.toml` file:

```
[dependencies]
autograd = "0.1"
```

Verification

Create a program to compute the derivative of a simple function:

```rust
use autograd as ag;
use autograd::tensor::Variable; // Import the Variable trait to
    use the `variable` method

fn main() {
    // Create a computational graph
    ag::with(|graph| {
        // Define a scalar variable x
        let x = graph.variable(ag::ndarray::arr0(3.0)); // x =
            3.0
        let y = x * x; // y = x^2

        // Compute the gradient of y with respect to x
        let grads = graph.grad(&[y], &[x]);

        // Handle the result from the gradient computation
        match grads[0].eval(&[]) {
            Ok(grad) => println!("Gradient of y with respect to
                x: {:?}", grad),
            Err(e) => println!("Error computing gradient: {:?}"
                , e),
        }
    });
}
```

Run the program and verify the gradient calculation:

```bash
$ cargo run
```

Expected Output

If `autograd` is installed and working correctly, the program will output:

```
Gradient of y with respect to x: 6.0 shape=[],
strides=[], layout=C | F (0x3), dynamic ndim=0
```

Explanation

- The program defines the function $y = x^2$.
- The gradient of y with respect to x is $\frac{dy}{dx} = 2x$.
- When $x = 3.0$, the gradient is $2 \times 3.0 = 6.0$.

If the output matches the expected result, the installation and usage of `autograd` are successful. If any errors occur, ensure the crate version in `Cargo.toml` is correct and recompile the project.

Installing and verifying these essential crates allows you to harness Rust's power for numerical computing, machine learning, and automatic differentiation. By integrating these libraries into your projects, you can build high-performance AI applications while benefiting from Rust's safety and speed.

2.4.6 Optimizing Rust for AI Workflows

Rust provides several features and configurations that can be optimized for AI workflows, enabling efficient data processing, model training, and debugging. Below are key areas to focus on:

2.4.6.1 Toolchain Configuration

Optimizing Rust's toolchain is essential for achieving high performance and efficient debugging in AI development.

- **Enable Performance Flags:** Use Cargo's `release` profile to enable compiler optimizations. Add the following configuration to your `Cargo.toml` file:

  ```
  [profile.release]
  opt-level = 3
  lto = ''thin''
  codegen-units = 1
  ```

  These settings enable maximum optimization level (`opt-level = 3`), apply `thin` link-time optimization for faster builds, and reduce the number of code generation units for more aggressive cross-function optimization.
  To actually use these optimizations, you must build or run your project with the `--release` flag:

  ```
  cargo build --release
  cargo run --release
  ```

  Without the `--release` flag, Cargo defaults to the `dev` profile, which prioritizes fast compilation over runtime performance.
  These settings enable maximum optimization (`opt-level = 3`), link-time optimization (`lto`), and a single code generation unit for better runtime performance.

- **Debugging Options:** During development, enable debug symbols by setting `debug = true` in the `Cargo.toml` file:

      [profile.dev]
      debug = true

  This ensures that debug information is available for troubleshooting without compromising development speed.
- **Use `cargo-watch`:** Install `cargo-watch` for automatically rebuilding and testing your project during development:

bash

```bash
$ cargo install cargo-watch
$ cargo watch -x run
```

  This reduces the manual overhead of recompilation and testing.

2.4.6.2 Managing Dependencies and Crate Versions

Maintaining up-to-date and compatible dependencies is crucial for projects involving large-scale data processing and model training. Follow these guidelines:

- **Update Dependencies Regularly:** Use the `cargo update` command to update dependencies to their latest compatible versions:

bash

```bash
$ cargo update
```

  Regular updates ensure your project benefits from the latest features and bug fixes.
- **Check for Compatibility Issues:** If updates introduce issues, review the dependency tree using:

bash

```bash
$ cargo tree
```

This command visualizes dependencies and highlights potential conflicts.

- **Managing Dependency Versions**:
  In the `Cargo.toml` file, you can specify version *ranges* or *exact versions* for each dependency. For example:

  ```
  [dependencies]
  ndarray = "0.15"
  linfa = "0.4"
  ```

  Although the syntax may appear to specify an exact version, the quotes indicate a **compatible version range**. In Cargo's semantic versioning system, `"0.15"` means "any version compatible with 0.15," i.e., any `0.15.x` release. This allows automatic patch-level updates (e.g., from `0.15.1` to `0.15.4`) while preventing breaking changes that might occur in `0.16` or higher.

  For crates that are **critical to your project's stability**, you may want to *pin* their versions to ensure full reproducibility. You can do this by using the = operator to specify an exact version:

  ```
  ndarray = "=0.15.4"
  ```

  Pinning is especially useful when a project relies on specific behavior or APIs that could change in future releases.

  Cargo also automatically maintains a **Cargo.lock** file, which records the exact versions of all dependencies (and their transitive dependencies) used during the last successful build. This ensures that future builds of the same project—on any system or CI pipeline—use identical versions. To preserve this reproducibility across collaborators and environments, it is good practice to **commit the Cargo.lock file to version control** (e.g., Git) along with your source code.

- **Handle Large-Scale Data Processing:** For AI workflows involving large datasets, leverage crates such as `rayon`, a lightweight data-parallelism library that simplifies converting sequential computations into parallel ones, ensuring data-race-free execution and adapting to runtime workloads, and `tokio`, a high-performance runtime for managing asynchronous tasks. Add these dependencies to your project and configure them appropriately to optimize your workflow.

bash

```bash
$ cargo add rayon
$ cargo add tokio
```

These crates improve efficiency and scalability in data-intensive tasks.

By configuring Rust's toolchain and managing dependencies effectively, you can optimize your workflows for AI development. Leveraging performance flags, debugging tools, and maintaining an updated dependency tree ensure stable and efficient project development, even for large-scale tasks.

Problems

2.1 Rust's `autograd` crate automates the computation of gradients. Write a Rust program using `autograd` to compute the derivative of the function $y = x^3$ at $x = 4.0$. Verify the output by calculating the derivative manually.

2.2 Installing and Verifying Crates: Add the `ndarray` crate to a Rust project and create an array [5, 10, 15]. Print the array to confirm successful installation.

2.3 Toolchain Configuration:

(a) Modify the `Cargo.toml` file to enable maximum optimization for release builds. Specify the settings required for `opt-level`, `lto`, and `codegen-units`.

(b) Run the command to build your project with these optimizations. How do the build times and performance differ between the development and release builds?

2.4 Managing Dependencies:
Use the `cargo update` command to update all dependencies in a Rust project. What command can you run to ensure that all dependencies were updated successfully?

Chapter 3
Rust Syntax for AI Practitioners (Optional)

3.1 Introduction

This chapter provides a concise introduction to the Rust programming language, tailored specifically for readers interested in applying Rust to deep learning and AI development. Rather than offering a complete tutorial, the chapter focuses on the essential syntax and concepts—such as ownership, borrowing, lifetimes, and memory safety—that differentiate Rust from other languages like Python and C++. It also touches on error handling, pattern matching, and basic data structures. While experienced Rust developers may choose to skip this chapter, it serves as a self-contained primer for readers coming from other programming backgrounds, particularly those familiar with Python or JavaScript. By the end, readers will have the foundational knowledge needed to understand and write idiomatic Rust code in subsequent deep learning chapters.

Chapter Goal

1. To provide a concise and practical introduction to Rust syntax for readers who may not be familiar with the language.
2. To explain key Rust concepts, such as ownership, borrowing, and memory safety.
3. To serve as an optional primer—experienced Rust developers may skip this chapter and proceed directly to the next.

3.2 Rust Syntax and Concepts

3.2.1 Basic Syntax

Understanding Rust's basic syntax and data types is essential for effectively leveraging the language in AI development. This section introduces the `println!` macro, explains variable mutability, and explores Rust's data types, including the distinction between signed and unsigned integers.

3.2.1.1 Understanding `println!` and Its Syntax

The `println!` macro is used in Rust to print output to the console. It is versatile, supporting formatted strings and dynamic placeholders.

© Mehrdad Maleki 2026
M. Maleki, *Deep Learning with Rust*, https://doi.org/10.1007/979-8-8688-2208-7_3

Syntax Explanation

```
println!("{}", variable);
```

- **println!**: A macro (indicated by the ! suffix) for sending formatted output to the standard output.
- **{}**: Placeholder for the value of a variable or expression.
- **variable**: The value to be inserted into the placeholder.

Example

```
1  let name = "Rust Programming";
2  println!("Welcome to {}", name);
```

Output

```
Welcome to Rust Programming
```

Multiple placeholders can be used for dynamic formatting:

```
1  println!("The temperature is {} C at {} AM.", 22, 8);
```

Output

```
The temperature is 22 C at 8 AM.
```

3.2.1.2   Variables, Constants, and Mutability

Rust variables are **immutable by default**, promoting clarity and preventing unintended changes to program state. It is important to note that immutability by default is not what guarantees memory safety—many memory-safe languages allow mutability—but rather a design choice that encourages more predictable and maintainable code. By limiting unnecessary mutation, Rust makes it easier to reason about program behavior, especially in concurrent or data-parallel settings where uncontrolled state changes can lead to errors and race conditions.

In Rust, `let` is used to create a new variable and assign it to a value. This, by default, create a mutable variable.

Immutable Variables

An immutable variable cannot be changed once assigned:

```
1  let x = 10; // Immutable
2  println!("Output: {}", x)
```

The output is:

```
Output: 10
```

But if you try to assign another value to x after the assignment, like this:

```
1  let x = 10; // Immutable
2  x=11;
3  println!("Output: {}", x)
```

You'll likely encounter an error message indicating that the variable is not mutable.

Mutable Variables

To allow changes, the `mut` keyword is used:

```rust
fn main() {
    let mut y = 20; // Mutable
    y += 5;
    println!("The updated value of y is: {}", y);
}
```

The output is:

```
The updated value of y is: 25
```

Constants

Constants are always immutable and must be explicitly typed. They are defined using the `const` keyword:

```rust
const PI: f64 = 3.14159;
println!("The value of PI is: {}", PI);
```

3.2.1.3 Primitive Data Types

Rust provides various primitive data types, ensuring efficient computation for AI workflows. These include:

Integers

Supports signed (`i8, i16, i32, i64`) and unsigned (`u8, u16, u32, u64`) integers. Example:

```rust
let a: i32 = 42;       // 32-bit signed integer
let b: u8 = 255;       // 8-bit unsigned integer

println!("Signed: {}, Unsigned: {}", a, b);
```

Floating-Point Numbers

Supports single-precision (`f32`) and double-precision (`f64`):

```rust
let score: f64 = 98.6;

println!("Score: {}", score);
```

Booleans and Characters

- **Booleans (`bool`):** Used for logical operations:

```rust
let is_active: bool = true;

println!("Is active: {}", is_active);
```

- **Characters (`char`):** Represent Unicode scalar values:

```rust
let symbol: char = 'A';

println!("Symbol: {}", symbol);
```

3.2.1.4   Signed and Unsigned Integers

Rust integers are categorized into signed and unsigned types based on their ability to represent negative numbers.

Signed Integers

- Represent both positive and negative values.
- Use the most significant bit (MSB) to indicate the sign:

  - 0 for positive values.
  - 1 for negative values.

- In Rust, signed integer types include `i8`, `i16`, `i32`, `i64`, and `i128`.
- Example for `i8`: range from -2^7 to $2^7 - 1$ (i.e., -128 to 127).

Signed integers in Rust are represented using the **two's complement** system. In this representation, the most significant bit acts as a sign indicator, but negative numbers are encoded by inverting all bits of their absolute value (the *one's complement*) and then adding 1. This design allows arithmetic operations (addition, subtraction, multiplication) to use the same binary circuitry for both positive and negative numbers without special handling.

   For example, in 8-bit two's complement:

- `0000 1101` represents $+13$.
- To represent -13, invert the bits to get `1111 0010` and add 1: `1111 0011`.
- Thus, `1111 0011` corresponds to -13.

This system has several advantages: it simplifies hardware design, ensures a unique representation for zero, and allows overflow behavior to wrap naturally in modular arithmetic.

Unsigned Integers

- Represent only nonnegative values.
- Use all bits for magnitude, allowing a larger positive range.
- Example for `u8`: 0 to $2^8 - 1$ (0 to 255).

Key Differences

- **Range**: Unsigned integers have a wider positive range than signed integers of the same size.
- **Use Cases**:

  - Signed integers (`i32`, `i64`) are used when negative values are required, such as in temperature calculations.
  - Unsigned integers (`u8`, `u16`, `u32`, `u64`, `u128`, and `usize`) represent only nonnegative values. They are commonly used when negative numbers are not meaningful, such as for counts or sizes. In Rust, however, only the `usize` type is used for array indexing and pointer arithmetic, as its size automatically matches the architecture of the target machine (32-bit or 64-bit).

Example

```rust
let signed_num: i8 = -10;   // Signed integer
let unsigned_num: u8 = 250; // Unsigned integer

println!("Signed: {}, Unsigned: {}", signed_num, unsigned_num);
```

Output

```
Signed: -10, Unsigned: 250
```

3.2.1.5   Strings and Slices

Efficient memory management is critical for handling strings in AI workflows. Rust provides two main string types: &str and String.

String Slices (&str)

A borrowed view of a string, allowing efficient and lightweight manipulation:

```rust
let greeting: &str = "Hello, Rust!";
println!("{}", greeting);
```

Owned Strings (String)

The String type in Rust represents an **owned**, heap-allocated, and growable UTF-8 string. It provides ownership over its contents, meaning the string's data is automatically freed when it goes out of scope. A String can be either mutable or immutable, depending on how it is declared—mutability is a property of the binding, not of the type itself.

```rust
let name = String::from("Rust");        // immutable binding
println!("{}", name);

let mut name = String::from("Rust");    // mutable binding
name.push_str(" Programming");
println!("{}", name);
```

In the first case, the variable name cannot be modified because it is immutable. In the second example, declaring it with mut allows methods like push_str() to modify the string in place.

Conversion Between &str and String

Conversion between these types is straightforward:

```rust
let s1: String = String::from("Deep Learning");
let s2: &str = &s1; // Borrow as a string slice

println!("Owned: {}, Slice: {}", s1, s2);
```

Output

```
Owned: Deep Learning, Slice: Deep Learning
```

This section introduced the foundational concepts of Rust, including the println! macro, variable mutability, data types, and the distinction between signed and unsigned integers. These concepts are fundamental for efficient AI application development in Rust.

3.2.2   Control Flow

Control flow and functions are essential components of programming in Rust, enabling decision-making, iteration, and modular code. This section introduces control structures and functions in Rust, emphasizing their syntax and use in AI applications.

Rust offers several control structures to manage the flow of execution in a program.

3.2.2.1   Conditional Statements: `if` and `else`

Syntax

```
if condition {
    // Code block executed if condition is true
} else {
    // Code block executed if condition is false
}
```

Example

```
1  let temperature = 30;
2
3  if temperature > 25 {
4      println!("It's hot outside.");
5  } else {
6      println!("It's a cool day.");
7  }
```

Output

```
It's hot outside.
```

3.2.2.2   Pattern Matching: `match`

Syntax

```
match value {
    pattern1 => action1,
    pattern2 => action2,
    _ => default_action,
}
```

_ acts as a wildcard for unmatched patterns.

Example

```
1  let value = 2;
2
3  match value {
4      1 => println!("One"),
5      2 => println!("Two"),
6      _ => println!("Something else"),
7  }
```

Output

```
Two
```

3.2.2.3 `loop`, `while`, and `for`

loop
Syntax

```rust
loop {
    // Infinite loop body
    if condition {
        break; // Exit the loop
    }
}
```

Example

```rust
let mut counter = 0;

loop {
    if counter == 3 {
        break;
    }
    println!("Counter: {}", counter);
    counter += 1;
}
```

Output

```
Counter: 0
Counter: 1
Counter: 2
```

3.2.2.4 `while`
Syntax

```rust
while condition {
    // Loop body executed as long as the condition is true
}
```

Example

```rust
let mut num = 5;

while num > 0 {
    println!("Counting down: {}", num);
    num -= 1;
}
```

Output

```
Counting down: 5
Counting down: 4
Counting down: 3
Counting down: 2
Counting down: 1
```

For Loops

A `for` loop in Rust iterates over elements of a collection or range:

```
1   for variable in collection {
2       // Loop body
3   }
```

For example, looping over a numeric range:

```
1   for i in 1..4 {
2       println!("Number: {}", i);
3   }
```

This loop prints the numbers 1, 2, and 3. The range syntax `1..4` is **exclusive** of the upper bound, meaning it includes 1, 2, and 3 but not 4. To include the upper bound, use the `..=` operator instead:

```
1   for i in 1..=4 {
2       println!("Number: {}", i); // prints 1, 2, 3, 4
3   }
```

3.2.3   Functions and Return Values

Functions in Rust can return values using either an explicit `return` statement or an implicit return, where the last expression in the function body is returned automatically.

```
1   fn add(a: i32, b: i32) -> i32 {
2       a + b // implicit return: no semicolon
3   }
4
5   fn main() {
6       let result = add(5, 3);
7       println!("The result is: {}", result);
8   }
```

Output

```
The result is: 8
```

In this example, the expression a + b is returned implicitly because it is the final line of the function and does not end with a semicolon. If you add a semicolon, the expression becomes a statement and will no longer return a value. You can also use an explicit return for clarity:

```
1  fn add(a: i32, b: i32) -> i32 {
2      return a + b; // explicit return
3  }
```

3.2.3.1 Closures

Closures are anonymous functions that capture variables from their enclosing scope.

Syntax

```
|parameters| {
    // Closure body
}
```

Example

```
1  let numbers = vec![1, 2, 3, 4];
2
3  let squared: Vec<i32> = numbers.iter().map(|x| x * x).collect()
       ;
4
5  println!("Squared values: {:?}", squared);
```

Output

```
Squared values: [1, 4, 9, 16]
```

- `numbers.iter()` creates an iterator over the vector.
- `(|x| x * x)` this is the closure.
- `.map(|x| x * x)` squares each element.
- `.collect()` gathers the results into a new `Vec<i32>` called `squared`.

This section introduced control structures (`if`, `else`, `match`, and loops) and functions in Rust, emphasizing their syntax and practical examples. Understanding these constructs is vital for implementing decision-making, iteration, and modular code in Rust.

3.3 Structs and Enums for Data Representation

In Rust, `structs` and `enums` are powerful tools for representing complex data. This section introduces `structs` for modeling complex data types and `enums` for handling data with multiple possible types or states.

3.3.1 Structs

`Structs` in Rust are used to create custom data types that group together related data fields. They are particularly useful in AI applications for representing layers in neural networks or datasets.

Syntax

```
struct StructName {
    field1: Type1,
    field2: Type2,
    ...
}
```

Structs: a minimal, idiomatic start (no enums yet)

```
1  #[derive(Debug)]
2  struct Layer {
3      name: &'static str,   // simple label; no heap allocs
4      units: usize,
5      uses_bias: bool,
6  }
7
8  fn main() {
9      let layer = Layer { name: "Hidden-1", units: 128, uses_bias
           : true };
10     println!("{:?}", layer);
11 }
```

Output

```
Layer: Hidden Layer 1, Neurons: 128, Activation: ReLU
```

3.3.2 Implementing Methods for Structs

You can define methods for a struct using the `impl` block:

```
1  impl StructName {
2      fn method_name(&self) -> ReturnType {
3          // Method body
4      }
5  }
```

The first parameter of every method is called `self`, which represents the instance the method is called on. Rust allows several forms of `self`, depending on how the method accesses or modifies the data:

- `&self` – Borrows the instance immutably; used when the method only reads data.
- `&mut self` – Borrows the instance mutably; used when the method modifies fields.
- `self` – Takes ownership of the instance; used when the method consumes the value.
- `Self` – Refers to the type itself (useful for constructors or associated functions).

For example:

```
1  struct Counter { value: i32 }
2
3  impl Counter {
4      fn get(&self) -> i32 { self.value }                    // read-only
```

```
5    fn increment(&mut self) { self.value += 1; } // modifies
         data
6    fn reset(self) -> i32 { self.value }          // consumes
         the instance
7  }
```

Example: Adding a Method to Calculate Total Parameters

```rust
struct Layer {
    name: String,
    num_neurons: usize,
    activation: String,
}

impl Layer {
    fn describe(&self) -> String {
        format!(
            "Layer: {}, Neurons: {}, Activation: {}",
            self.name, self.num_neurons, self.activation
        )
    }
}

fn main() {
    let layer = Layer {
        name: String::from("Output Layer"),
        num_neurons: 10,
        activation: String::from("Softmax"),
    };

    println!("{}", layer.describe());
}
```

Output

```
Layer: Output Layer, Neurons: 10, Activation: Softmax
```

The describe() method is defined as part of the impl Layer block, and it formats the properties of the Layer instance into a string. When you call layer.describe(), it generates a human-readable description of the layer.

3.3.2.1 Enums with Associated Data

Enums can hold additional data in their variants, making them versatile for representing complex types and states.

Syntax

```
enum EnumName {
    Variant1(Type),
    Variant2 { field1: Type1, field2: Type2 },
}
```

```rust
enum Activation {
    ReLU,
    Sigmoid,
    Tanh,
}

fn describe_activation(activation: Activation) {
    match activation {
        Activation::ReLU => println!("Rectified Linear Unit"),
        Activation::Sigmoid => println!("Sigmoid Activation"),
        Activation::Tanh => println!("Hyperbolic Tangent"),
    }
}

fn main() {
    let activations = [
        Activation::ReLU,
        Activation::Sigmoid,
        Activation::Tanh,
    ];

    for act in activations {
        describe_activation(act);
    }
}
```

Output

```
Rectified Linear Unit
Sigmoid Activation
Hyperbolic Tangent
```

This section introduced `structs` and `enums`, two essential tools for data representation in Rust. `Structs` provide a way to define and manipulate complex data types, while `enums` enable handling multiple data states or categories effectively. Both constructs are invaluable for designing robust AI models and managing data workflows.

3.4 Error Handling

Rust provides robust mechanisms for handling errors, ensuring safe and predictable execution. In this section, we explore the `Result` and `Option` types for managing errors effectively, particularly in AI workflows where issues such as missing data or incompatible types are common.

3.4.1   The Result Type

The Result type is used for operations that can either succeed or fail. It is defined as:

```
enum Result<T, E> {
    Ok(T),
    Err(E),
}
```

Here, T represents the type of value returned upon success, and E represents the error type.

Error Handling with the Result Type

This example demonstrates how to use the Result type to handle potential division errors:[1]

```rust
fn safe_division(a: f64, b: f64) -> Result<f64, String> {
    if b == 0.0 {
        Err(String::from("Division by zero"))
    } else {
        Ok(a / b)
    }
}

fn main() {
    match safe_division(10.0, 0.0) {
        Ok(result) => println!("Result: {}", result),
        Err(e) => println!("Error: {}", e),
    }
}
```

Output

```
Error: Division by zero
```

3.4.2   The Option Type

The Option type is used for values that might be absent. It is defined as:

```
enum Option<T> {
    Some(T),
    None,
}
```

---

[1] Rust's standard library already provides a built-in function for safe floating-point division: f64::checked_div().
This method returns an Option<f64>, yielding None when dividing by zero and Some(result) otherwise. For
example, 10.0f64.checked_div(0.0) evaluates to None. This difference between Option (which represents
"something or nothing") and Result (which represents "success or error") is central to Rust's approach to robust
error handling. Both types provide useful helper methods such as unwrap(), expect(), map(), and and_then() that
make error propagation concise and expressive.

Example: Handling Missing Data

This example demonstrates how to handle missing data using the `Option` type:

```rust
fn get_value(data: Option<i32>) {
    match data {
        Some(value) => println!("Value: {}", value),
        None => println!("No value found"),
    }
}

fn main() {
    let present = Some(42);
    let missing: Option<i32> = None;

    get_value(present);
    get_value(missing);
}
```

This will output:

```
Value: 42
No value found
```

3.4.3   Error Propagation and the ? Operator

AI workflows often encounter specific errors, such as missing data or incompatible types. Rust's `Result` type and the ? operator make it straightforward to handle and propagate such errors.

```rust
fn parse_and_add(a: &str, b: &str) -> Result<i32, String> {
    let num_a: i32 = a.parse().map_err(|_| "Invalid number".
        to_string())?;
    let num_b: i32 = b.parse().map_err(|_| "Invalid number".
        to_string())?;
    Ok(num_a + num_b)
}

fn main() {
    match parse_and_add("42", "x") {
        Ok(result) => println!("Result: {}", result),
        Err(e) => println!("Error: {}", e),
    }
}
```

Output

```
Error: Invalid number
```

The ? operator is a convenient shorthand for propagating errors. When used after a function call that returns a `Result`, it automatically:

- Returns the `Ok` value if the operation succeeds, or
- Returns the `Err` value immediately from the enclosing function if an error occurs.

In other words, this line:

```
1  let num_a: i32 = a.parse().map_err(|_| "Invalid number".
       to_string())?;
```

is equivalent to:

```
1  let num_a: i32 = match a.parse().map_err(|_| "Invalid number".
       to_string()) {
2      Ok(value) => value,
3      Err(e) => return Err(e),
4  };
```

The `?` operator simplifies error propagation without obscuring control flow, making it ideal for building robust AI data-processing pipelines where many operations can fail gracefully.

3.4.4   Best Practices for Error Handling

Use unwrap and expect Cautiously

The `unwrap` and `expect` methods are convenient for quickly extracting values from `Option` or `Result` types. However, if the value is `None` or `Err`, these methods will cause a program panic. This can lead to crashes that are difficult to debug, especially in production. Instead, prefer using `match` or the `?` operator for more robust error handling, allowing your program to gracefully handle failures and continue execution where appropriate.

Document Error Types for Functions Returning Result

When a function returns a `Result`, it is essential to document the types of errors it may produce. This practice not only improves code readability but also helps other developers understand the possible failure scenarios of your function. Clear documentation of error types aids in debugging and ensures that error handling is implemented correctly wherever the function is used.

Using Enums for Error Types Rust's `enum` type is particularly well suited for representing custom error categories. Each variant can describe a distinct kind of failure, often carrying additional context or data. This approach makes your error handling both explicit and extensible.

```
1  #[derive(Debug)]
2  enum ParseError {
3      EmptyInput,
4      InvalidFormat,
5      OutOfRange,
6  }
7
8  fn parse_number(s: &str) -> Result<i32, ParseError> {
9      if s.is_empty() {
10          return Err(ParseError::EmptyInput);
11      }
```

```
12      let num: i32 = s.parse().map_err(|_| ParseError::
            InvalidFormat)?;
13      if num < 0 {
14          return Err(ParseError::OutOfRange);
15      }
16      Ok(num)
17  }
18
19  fn main() {
20      match parse_number("-42") {
21          Ok(n) => println!("Parsed number: {}", n),
22          Err(e) => println!("Error: {:?}", e),
23      }
24  }
```

Output

```
Error: OutOfRange
```

By defining custom error enums, you make it clear what kinds of failures can occur, improve
debuggability, and create a strong foundation for robust error handling across larger AI systems.

Leverage Option for Optional Values

In many programs, certain values may or may not be present—such as missing data, incomplete
user input, or uninitialized states. Rust models this explicitly using the Option<T> type, which can
be either Some(value) or None. This eliminates the need for special sentinel values (e.g., -1 or 0)
that carry additional meaning beyond their actual numeric value.

While the borrow checker ensures memory safety and prevents null pointer dereferences, the
Option type prevents the logical errors that arise from ambiguous or invalid data representations.

For example:

```
1   fn find_max(numbers: &[i32]) -> Option<i32> {
2       if numbers.is_empty() {
3           None
4       } else {
5           Some(*numbers.iter().max().unwrap())
6       }
7   }
8
9   fn main() {
10      let values = vec![3, 7, 2];
11      match find_max(&values) {
12          Some(max) => println!("Maximum value: {}", max),
13          None => println!("No values provided"),
14      }
15  }
```

Output

```
Maximum value: 7
```

The `Option` type encourages explicit handling of the "no value" case, leading to safer and more readable code. You can combine it with methods such as `map()`, `and_then()`, or `unwrap_or()` to express optional logic concisely without resorting to manual `if` checks.

3.5 Memory Safety in AI Workflows

Rust enforces memory safety at compile time through its ownership model and borrow checker. These mechanisms prevent common errors such as dangling pointers, buffer overflows, or double frees, which can lead to undefined behavior and subtle data corruption.

In the context of AI, memory safety provides significant practical advantages. AI workflows often manipulate large datasets, tensors, or model parameters in memory-intensive environments. In memory-unsafe languages such as C or C++, a single invalid pointer dereference or use-after-free bug can silently corrupt training data, cause segmentation faults during long-running experiments, or produce incorrect model outputs that are difficult to trace. Such issues may not surface immediately, leading to unreliable results or wasted computation.

By enforcing memory safety at compile time, Rust eliminates entire classes of runtime errors without sacrificing performance. While this requires developers to work within stricter ownership and borrowing rules, the trade-off is highly worthwhile: AI systems built in Rust are more robust, reproducible, and less prone to catastrophic failures in production. This balance between performance and safety makes Rust a compelling alternative to C++ for high-performance AI applications.

Example: Safely Managing Large Datasets
The following example demonstrates how Rust manages ownership when working with large datasets:

```rust
fn process_dataset(data: Vec<i32>) {
    println!("Processing dataset with {} elements", data.len())
        ;
    // Ownership of 'data' ends here
}

fn main() {
    let dataset = vec![1, 2, 3, 4, 5];
    process_dataset(dataset);
    // dataset cannot be accessed here as ownership is moved
    // println!("{:?}", dataset); // Uncommenting this will
        cause a compile error
}
```

The output is:

```
Processing dataset with 5 elements
```

In this example, ownership of the dataset is transferred to the `process_dataset` function, ensuring that the dataset is not accessed after processing.

3.5.1 Borrowing and References

Borrowing in Rust allows parts of a program to access data without taking ownership, using either immutable or mutable references. This concept extends beyond functions—it applies to closures, loops, and other code blocks where multiple parts of a program need temporary access to the same data. Borrowing is particularly valuable in AI applications, where large datasets or model parameters must be shared safely across multiple processing stages without unnecessary copying.

Immutable and Mutable Borrowing in Practice

Rust's borrowing rules distinguish between immutable references (&T) and mutable references (&mut T). You can have multiple immutable borrows at the same time, but only one mutable borrow to a given piece of data at any moment. This design prevents data races and ensures thread and memory safety at compile time.

The following example demonstrates both immutable and mutable borrowing when working with datasets—an essential operation in AI workflows where data must often be read and modified efficiently without duplication:

```rust
fn calculate_sum(data: &Vec<i32>) -> i32 {
    // Immutable borrow: only reading data
    data.iter().sum()
}

fn update_first_element(data: &mut Vec<i32>, value: i32) {
    // Mutable borrow: temporarily allows modification
    if let Some(first) = data.get_mut(0) {
        *first = value;
    }
}

fn main() {
    let mut dataset = vec![1, 2, 3, 4, 5];

    // Immutable borrow: safe because we're only reading
    println!("Sum: {}", calculate_sum(&dataset));

    // Mutable borrow: temporarily grants write access
    update_first_element(&mut dataset, 10);

    // After the mutable borrow ends, we can read again
    println!("Updated dataset: {:?}", dataset);

    // We can also borrow immutably again without issues
    println!("New sum: {}", calculate_sum(&dataset));
}
```

Output

```
Sum: 15
Updated dataset: [10, 2, 3, 4, 5]
New sum: 24
```

This example highlights how Rust's borrowing rules allow efficient, concurrent-safe access to shared data without copying. Immutable references let multiple parts of a program read data freely, while mutable references provide controlled, exclusive write access. These guarantees make Rust ideal for data-heavy AI workflows, where datasets are large and concurrent access must remain safe and predictable.

A Note on Lifetimes

Rust's compiler tracks how long references remain valid through a feature called **lifetimes**. While lifetimes are an essential part of Rust's memory safety guarantees, they are a more advanced topic best understood after becoming comfortable with ownership and borrowing. We will revisit lifetimes in detail later, where we will explore how they prevent dangling references and enable safe, efficient data sharing. Curious readers can find more information about lifetimes in the official Rust documentation at https://doc.rust-lang.org/book/ch10-03-lifetime-syntax.html.

3.5.2   Memory Allocation and Deallocation

Rust provides tools like `Box`, `Rc`, and `Arc` for heap allocation and shared ownership, which are critical for handling large neural networks or datasets in AI.

Box: Single Ownership

Box<T> is the simplest smart pointer in Rust and provides single ownership with heap allocation. It allows data to be stored on the heap while a fixed-size pointer to that data remains on the stack, enabling the compiler to know the size of the type at compile time. This is particularly important for recursive data structures (such as trees or linked lists), whose size would otherwise be infinite. Box<T> introduces no performance overhead beyond heap allocation and is commonly used when a type's size cannot be known at compile time, when transferring ownership of large data without copying, or when owning a value abstractly via a trait rather than a concrete type.

```rust
fn main() {
    let boxed_value = Box::new(42);
    println!("Boxed value: {}", boxed_value);
}
```

Rc: Shared Ownership

```rust
use std::rc::Rc;

fn main() {
    let shared_data = Rc::new(vec![1, 2, 3]);

    // Clone the reference using the dot syntax (more idiomatic)
    let clone1 = shared_data.clone();
    let clone2 = shared_data.clone();

    println!("Reference count: {}", Rc::strong_count(&
        shared_data));
}
```

Output

```
Reference count: 3
```

Rust allows both `Rc::clone(&value)` and `value.clone()` to create new reference-counted pointers. The two forms are functionally equivalent, but the dot syntax (`value.clone()`) is more idiomatic because it reads naturally and is consistent with how cloning is done for other types. The explicit form (`Rc::clone(&value)`) is often used in documentation or educational examples to make it clear that cloning an Rc only copies the reference, not the underlying data.

- **Rc<T>**: A smart pointer in Rust that provides reference counting for shared ownership. It is used when multiple parts of the program need to share ownership of the same data.
- **Rc::new**: Creates a new instance of Rc<T> to wrap the given data.
- **Rc::clone**: Creates a new reference to the same data, incrementing the reference count.
- **Rc::strong_count**: Returns the number of strong references to the data.

This example demonstrates how Rc allows multiple references to share ownership of the same vector, and the reference count reflects the number of owners.

The output shows that the reference count for the shared data is 3, as the original Rc and its two clones are all pointing to the same data.

Arc: Thread-Safe Shared Ownership

```rust
use std::sync::Arc;
use std::thread;

fn main() {
    let shared_data = Arc::new(vec![1, 2, 3]);
    let threads: Vec<_> = (0..3)
        .map(|_| {
            let data = Arc::clone(&shared_data);
            thread::spawn(move || {
                println!("Thread data: {:?}", data);
            })
        })
        .collect();

    for t in threads {
        t.join().unwrap();
    }
}
```

Output

```
Thread data: [1, 2, 3]
Thread data: [1, 2, 3]
Thread data: [1, 2, 3]
```

- **Arc<T>**: A thread-safe smart pointer that allows multiple threads to share ownership of the same data.
- **Arc::new**: Creates a new instance of Arc<T> to wrap the given data.
- **Arc::clone**: Clones the Arc, incrementing the reference count, and shares ownership with another thread.

- **`thread::spawn`**: Creates a new thread to execute the given closure. The `move` keyword ensures the thread takes ownership of the captured variables.
- **`t.join()`**: Blocks the main thread until the spawned thread completes.

This code safely shares ownership of the vector across multiple threads. Each thread prints the shared data, demonstrating thread-safe access with no risk of data races.

The use of `Arc` ensures safe and efficient handling of shared data across multiple threads. Rust's combination of memory safety guarantees and tools like `Arc` makes it an excellent choice for concurrent programming, particularly in AI workflows requiring large-scale data handling.

Rust's memory safety guarantees, combined with its tools for ownership, borrowing, and heap allocation, make it an excellent choice for AI applications. These features enable developers to handle large datasets and models efficiently while ensuring code safety and reliability.

3.6   The Ownership Model for Data Handling

Rust's ownership model is a foundational feature that ensures memory safety and eliminates common bugs like null pointer dereferences or data races. In AI workflows, ownership principles enable efficient and safe handling of large datasets and models.

3.6.1   The Ownership Concept in Rust

Rust's ownership model is distinct from traditional garbage collection systems. In Rust:

- Each value in memory has a single owner.
- When the owner goes out of scope, the value is automatically dropped.
- Ownership is transferred (moved) when assigning or passing values.

Benefits of Ownership
The ownership model provides:

- Improved performance by avoiding the overhead of garbage collection.
- Enhanced memory safety by preventing use-after-free or double-free errors.

3.6.2   Clone and Copy Traits

Both `Copy` and `Clone` produce a duplicate of a value, but they differ in *how* duplication happens and when it is triggered.

- **`Copy`** is a marker trait for types that can be duplicated by a simple byte-for-byte copy of their in-memory representation (no custom logic, no heap allocation). If a type is `Copy`, assignments and function calls *implicitly* copy the value instead of moving it. A type can be `Copy` only if *all* its fields are `Copy`, and a `Copy` type cannot implement `Drop`. Examples: `i32`, `f64`, `bool`, `char`, tuples/arrays of `Copy` types (e.g., `(i32, i32)`, `[u8; 16]`).
- **`Clone`** provides an `clone()` method for *explicit* duplication and may perform arbitrary work (e.g., allocate and copy heap data). Many non-`Copy` owners like `String`, `Vec<T>`, and `Box<T>` implement `Clone` to duplicate their owned resources.

Important Distinctions

- `Copy` $\Rightarrow$ `Clone`: Every `Copy` type is also `Clone` (the compiler provides a trivial `clone()` that does a bitwise copy).

- "Deep vs. shallow" is *not* guaranteed by the trait name: Clone's semantics are type specific. For example, String::clone() duplicates the heap buffer (deep), but Rc::clone() only increments the reference count (not a deep copy of the pointee).
- A type can be Copy even if it's a "complex struct," provided all fields are Copy (i.e., trivially bytewise-copyable). Ownership of heap data (e.g., String, Vec<T>) prevents Copy.

Example: Using Clone and Copy

```rust
fn main() {
    let x = 42; // i32 implements Copy
    let y = x; // Copy occurs here
    println!("x: {}, y: {}", x, y);

    let s1 = String::from("Deep Learning");
    let s2 = s1.clone(); // Clone creates a deep copy
    println!("s1: {}, s2: {}", s1, s2);
}
```

The output is as follows:

```
x: 42, y: 42
s1: Deep Learning, s2: Deep Learning
```

Rule of Thumb If you want automatic, zero-overhead duplication on assignment/argument passing, design your type so all fields are Copy. Otherwise, provide an explicit, well-defined Clone that does exactly the duplication your type needs (deep when appropriate).

3.6.3   Using Ownership in AI Workflows

Ownership principles can streamline AI workflows by ensuring efficient data handling and reducing runtime errors.

Practical Example: Neural Network Pipeline

```rust
struct Layer {
    name: String,
    neurons: usize,
}

fn build_pipeline() -> Vec<Layer> {
    vec![
        Layer { name: String::from("Input Layer"), neurons: 64
            },
        Layer { name: String::from("Hidden Layer"), neurons:
            128 },
        Layer { name: String::from("Output Layer"), neurons: 10
            },
    ]
}
```

```
13
14  fn main() {
15      let pipeline = build_pipeline();
16      for layer in pipeline {
17          println!("Layer: {}, Neurons: {}", layer.name, layer.
                neurons);
18      }
19  }
```

Output

```
Layer: Input Layer, Neurons: 64
Layer: Hidden Layer, Neurons: 128
Layer: Output Layer, Neurons: 10
```

Explanation

This example demonstrates how Rust's ownership and borrowing system ensures safe and efficient handling of data in AI workflows. The `build_pipeline` function creates a vector of `Layer` instances, each representing a stage in a neural network pipeline. Ownership of the pipeline vector is transferred to the `main` function, where it is safely used and automatically dropped when it goes out of scope.

It is important to note, however, that ownership alone does not prevent memory leaks—safe Rust can still leak memory intentionally (e.g., through reference cycles or by using `std::mem::forget`). What actually prevents dangling references and unsafe memory access is the **borrow checker**, which enforces Rust's strict rules on how data can be accessed, shared, or modified.

In the loop `for layer in pipeline`, each `Layer` is moved (its ownership is transferred temporarily) and used safely without the risk of invalid access. After the loop, all layers are dropped in a controlled and predictable manner, ensuring memory safety and eliminating common issues such as use-after-free or data races that occur in memory-unsafe languages.

Summary

This chapter has provided a foundation in Rust's syntax, memory management, and ownership model, highlighting their importance in AI development. This knowledge is essential for building safe, efficient AI applications, setting the stage for more advanced Rust-based AI projects in the following chapters.

Problems

3.1 Ownership and Borrowing Basics: Define a function `consume_text(text: String)` that prints the input string. In the `main` function, create a `String` called message = `String::from("Rust is great!")`, pass it to `consume_text`, and then try to print it again in `main`. Observe the compiler error. Next, modify `consume_text` to take `&str` as input, and verify that `message` is still usable afterward.

3.2 Mutable vs. Immutable References: Create a mutable integer variable `counter = 0`. Write a function `increment(x: &mut i32)` that adds 1 to the given value. In `main`, pass `&mut counter` to `increment` and print the result. Then, try to pass `&counter` (an immutable reference) and observe the compiler error.

3.3 Pattern Matching with `match`: Write a function `describe_number(n: i32) -> &'static str` that returns:

- `"zero"` if n `==` 0
- `"positive"` if n `>` 0
- `"negative"` if n `<` 0

In `main`, call the function for -7, 0, and 42 and print the results.

3.4 Working with Enums and Structs: Define an enum Shape with variants:

- `Circle(f64)`
- `Rectangle(f64, f64)`

Then write a function `area(s: Shape) -> f64` that calculates the area:

- Circle: πr^2
- Rectangle: $w \times h$

In `main`, calculate and print the area of `Circle(3.0)` and `Rectangle(4.0, 2.5)`.

3.5 Using Iterators with Vectors: Create a vector `numbers = vec![1, 2, 3, 4, 5]`. Use `iter().map()` to square each element and collect the results into a new vector `squares`. Print both `numbers` and `squares`.

Chapter 4
Why Rust for Deep Learning?

4.1 Introduction

This chapter outlines why Rust is a compelling choice for deep learning. We focus on Rust's core strengths—performance, memory safety, and concurrency—and how they address key limitations in Python-based workflows. By emphasizing low-level control, zero-cost abstractions, and data-race-free parallelism, Rust enables faster and safer execution for compute-heavy tasks common in machine learning.

Chapter Goal

1. Explain Rust's core strengths—performance, memory safety, and concurrency—in the context of deep learning.
2. Compare Rust's execution model to Python's, focusing on control, predictability, and overhead.
3. Highlight how Rust's language features reduce runtime errors and improve computational efficiency in ML pipelines.

4.2 Why Rust?

The unique features of Rust—such as ownership, lifetimes, and strict scope enforcement—make it an excellent choice for building deep learning systems. In this short chapter, we explore the reasons why Rust is well suited for deep learning applications and compare its core efficiency with more commonly used language like Python.

Since Python share many design goals with other languages, the insights provided here will also help curious readers draw broader comparisons between Rust and those ecosystems.

4.3 Lifetime and Scope in Rust and Their Importance in Deep Learning

In this section, we examine how Rust's concepts of lifetime and scope contribute to safe and efficient memory management—critical for high-performance deep learning systems.

In Python, the lifetime of a variable is determined by its scope. Python uses dynamic memory management: when a variable goes out of scope, it becomes eligible for garbage collection. While convenient, garbage collection introduces unpredictable latency and overhead on the CPU and

© Mehrdad Maleki 2026
M. Maleki, *Deep Learning with Rust*, https://doi.org/10.1007/979-8-8688-2208-7_4

memory, which can negatively impact the performance of deep learning applications where speed is paramount.

Python variables fall into three primary scopes:

- **Local:** The variable is only accessible within the function or block where it is defined.
- **Global:** The variable is accessible throughout the program.
- **Enclosing:** The variable is defined in a surrounding (non-global) scope and is accessible within nested functions (closures).

Rust, on the other hand, offers *fine-grained control over lifetimes and scopes*. A variable's lifetime in Rust begins when it is created and ends when it is destroyed, and this is explicitly managed at compile time by the **borrow checker**. While scope determines where a variable can be accessed, **lifetimes** ensure that all references to data remain valid for as long as they are used.

Consider borrowing in Rust using the & symbol. The lifetime of a borrow is defined by the block in which it is declared and is enforced to end before the original owner is destroyed. The compiler checks this at compile time, thus preventing use-after-free errors and data races. This safety comes with a slight increase in complexity for the developer but leads to much more efficient and predictable memory behavior.

Unlike Python's garbage collector, which periodically frees memory during execution, Rust guarantees that memory is freed immediately and deterministically when a variable goes out of scope. This leads to lower runtime overhead and more consistent performance, especially in compute-intensive applications like deep learning.

For example, suppose we load an image as input to a neural network. In Python, the image object will stay in memory until garbage collection decides to clean it up. In Rust, once the image is passed into a processing function (such as a neural network layer implementation), and that function completes, the image's memory is immediately freed—unless explicitly returned or moved elsewhere. This guarantees efficient use of system resources.

4.4 Performance Advantages of Rust in Deep Learning

Rust is a statically typed, compiled language that produces highly optimized machine code at compile time. Unlike Python, which interprets code dynamically and often delegates performance-critical tasks to external C libraries, Rust provides native high performance with full developer control over memory layout and execution.

4.4.1 Why Rust Is Faster

- **No Interpreter Overhead:** Rust code is compiled directly to machine instructions, while Python introduces overhead through its interpreter.
- **No Global Interpreter Lock (GIL):** Python's GIL restricts concurrent execution of threads, especially on multi-core CPUs. Rust, on the other hand, allows true multi-threading with zero-cost synchronization when safe.
- **Zero-Cost Abstractions:** Rust's abstractions (such as iterators, closures, and ownership) are designed to be *zero-cost*—i.e., they can usually be compiled away with no runtime overhead. In practice, this means that high-level Rust code can achieve performance comparable to handwritten low-level code. However, this relies on the compiler being able to recognize and optimize these patterns, so while most abstractions are optimized out, in certain cases some minor overhead may remain.

- **Efficient Memory Access:** Rust gives fine-grained control over data structures and avoids indirection (common in Python), enabling faster memory access and lower cache misses.

4.4.2 Example: CSV Data Preprocessing

Suppose we want to load a large CSV file and normalize all numeric columns.

In Python (with Pandas)

```python
import pandas as pd

df = pd.read_csv("data.csv")
df = (df - df.mean()) / df.std()
```

This code is elegant but under the hood:

- It uses Python's dynamic typing and runtime reflection.
- Memory usage is often higher due to unnecessary copies.
- Performance depends on underlying C/C++ implementation in Pandas/NumPy.

In Rust (with ndarray and csv crates)

```rust
use csv::Reader;
use std::error::Error;
use std::fs::File;

fn main() -> Result<(), Box<dyn Error>> {
    let file = File::open("data.csv")?;
    let mut rdr = Reader::from_reader(file);

    for result in rdr.records() {
        let record = result?;
        println!("{:?}", record);
    }

    Ok(())
}
```

This version:

- Avoids intermediate allocations and operates on raw memory.
- Benefits from SIMD and loop unrolling via LLVM.
- Can process millions of rows in parallel using Rayon or threads.

4.5 Concurrency and Parallelism in Rust for AI Workloads

Parallelism is increasingly critical in AI workloads, especially in tasks like data preprocessing, augmentation, model evaluation, and distributed training. While Python is the most widely used language in AI today, its concurrency model is limited by the Global Interpreter Lock (GIL), which

Table 4.1 Rust vs. Python performance for computing the sum of squares of 10^6 integers

Language	Mode	Execution time (sec)	Speedup vs. Rust serial	Notes
Rust	Serial	0.0145	1.00×	Efficient native code with zero-cost abstractions
Rust	Parallel	0.0019	**7.64×**	Multithreaded with Rayon; minimal overhead, full CPU utilization
Python	Serial	0.0510	0.28×	Slower due to dynamic typing and interpreted execution
Python	Parallel	>600	<0.00002×	GIL and process pickling significantly reduce performance

prevents multiple threads from executing Python bytecode in parallel. This significantly restricts Python's ability to utilize multi-core CPUs effectively in native code.

Rust, on the other hand, offers **zero-cost, thread-safe parallelism** through its strong compile-time guarantees. Using constructs like `std::thread`, `Arc`, `Mutex`, and high-level parallel iterators from the `rayon` crate, developers can build concurrent AI systems without worrying about data races or memory corruption.

4.5.1   Performance Comparison: Rust vs. Python for Parallel Computation

In this section, we compare Rust and Python in a basic numeric computation task—computing the sum of squares from 0 to 1,000,000—using both serial and parallel approaches. The purpose is to highlight the real-world performance benefits Rust offers due to its compile-time optimizations, memory safety, and efficient multi-threading support via the Rayon crate. By contrast, Python suffers from performance limitations due to its interpreted nature and multiprocessing overhead (Table 4.1).

4.5.2   Benchmark Results

4.5.3   Rust Code

Listing 4.1   Parallel and serial sum in rust with rayon

```rust
use rayon::prelude::*;
use std::time::Instant;

fn square(x: u64) -> u64 {
    x * x
}

fn main() {
    let n: u64 = 1_000_000;
    let data: Vec<u64> = (0..n).collect();

```

```rust
12      let start = Instant::now();
13      let _sum_serial: u64 = data.iter().map(|&x| square(x)).sum
           ();
14      let duration_serial = start.elapsed();
15      println!("Serial time: {:.6} sec", duration_serial.
           as_secs_f64());
16
17      let start = Instant::now();
18      let _sum_parallel: u64 = data.par_iter().map(|&x| square(x)
           ).sum();
19      let duration_parallel = start.elapsed();
20      println!("Parallel time: {:.6} sec", duration_parallel.
           as_secs_f64());
21
22      let speedup = duration_serial.as_secs_f64() /
           duration_parallel.as_secs_f64();
23      println!("Speedup: {:.2}x", speedup);
24  }
```

4.5.4   How Parallelism Works in Rust

The core of Rust's performance advantage in parallel computation lies in its thread-safe, zero-cost abstraction provided by the `rayon` crate (Listing 4.1).

- **`par_iter()`** turns a collection into a parallel iterator that splits data into chunks.
- These chunks are distributed across a thread pool managed by Rayon, leveraging all available CPU cores.
- Each thread computes the square of its assigned numbers independently using `map()`.
- After mapping, a **parallel reduction** (`sum()`) aggregates the results.
- Rayon automatically balances workloads using work stealing, ensuring all threads stay busy.

4.5.5   Python Code

Listing 4.2 demonstrates a comparison between serial and parallel execution in Python by computing a sum sequentially and using the multiprocessing module to parallelize the same operation.

Listing 4.2 Parallel and serial sum in python

```python
1  import time
2  from multiprocessing import Pool
3
4  def square(x):
5      return x * x
6
7  if __name__ == "__main__":
8      data = list(range(1_000_000))
```

```
 9
10      start = time.time()
11      _sum_serial = sum(square(x) for x in data)
12      duration_serial = time.time() - start
13      print(f"Serial time: {duration_serial:.6f} sec")
14
15      start = time.time()
16      with Pool() as pool:
17          _sum_parallel = sum(pool.map(square, data))
18      duration_parallel = time.time() - start
19      print(f"Parallel time: {duration_parallel:.6f} sec")
```

4.5.6　CPU Parallelism in the Age of GPU Compute

While most deep learning training workloads today are GPU-bound, multi-threaded CPU computation remains highly relevant in modern AI systems. CPU parallelism plays a critical role in data preprocessing, feature extraction, input/output (I/O) operations, and orchestration of GPU workloads. Efficient CPU-side code ensures that GPUs remain fully utilized by minimizing bottlenecks in data loading, augmentation, and model evaluation pipelines. Rust's ability to express safe, low-overhead parallelism—without the runtime penalties of Python's multiprocessing or the Global Interpreter Lock (GIL)—makes it exceptionally well suited for building these performance-critical components of deep learning infrastructures.

4.6　Tooling and Ecosystem in Rust for Deep Learning

While Python currently dominates the AI space with mature libraries like `TensorFlow` and `PyTorch`, Rust's ecosystem is rapidly evolving to meet the demands of performance-critical machine learning applications. Several promising Rust libraries are gaining traction, offering differentiable programming, GPU acceleration, and model-building tools that leverage Rust's strengths in performance and safety.

4.6.1　Emerging Libraries in Rust

- **Burn:** A modular deep learning framework designed for performance, usability, and flexibility. It supports both CPU and GPU back ends and provides a clear abstraction over training loops, optimizers, and neural network layers.
- **Autograd.rs:** A lightweight automatic differentiation engine for Rust that enables gradient-based optimization without macro-heavy overhead. Ideal for learning and experimentation with custom models.
- **Autodiff**: A lightweight crate that provides forward-mode automatic differentiation in Rust. It is especially useful for implementing gradient descent, custom loss functions, and testing differentiable mathematical operations. The syntax is minimal and intuitive.

Table 4.2 Comparison of python and rust for deep learning

Feature	Python	Rust
Speed	Moderate (depends heavily on C-based libraries like NumPy)	Very High (native execution, zero-cost abstractions)
Memory Management	Garbage collected (automatic, but with overhead)	Ownership-based (no GC, deterministic, faster)
Concurrency	Limited (GIL restricts true multi-threading)	Thread-safe by design (no GIL, native threading, data race prevention)
Tooling for AI	Mature (PyTorch, TensorFlow, scikit-learn)	Growing (Burn, Candle, Linfa, Autograd.rs)
Learning Curve	Easy for beginners	Moderate (requires understanding ownership and lifetimes)

- **Candle:** A minimalist, high-performance deep learning library inspired by PyTorch, but optimized for Rust's zero-cost abstractions. It emphasizes simplicity and speed and is used in real-world LLM and inference scenarios.
- **Linfa:** A general-purpose classical machine learning toolkit for tasks like clustering, SVM, and regression, similar to scikit-learn.

These libraries give developers low-level control over the internals of models and memory usage. This is particularly useful in AI research, embedded systems, and production inference environments where performance and reliability are paramount.

Summary

In this chapter, we examined the core advantages of using Rust over Python for deep learning. Python's ease of use and mature libraries make it ideal for prototyping, but its runtime limitations—including garbage collection and the Global Interpreter Lock (GIL)—create bottlenecks in performance-critical tasks.

In contrast, Rust offers precise memory control, thread-safe concurrency, and high-speed execution without sacrificing safety. We highlighted how these features can significantly speed up CSV parsing, matrix operations, and custom model logic, reducing runtime errors and resource usage.

With growing support through libraries like autodiff, Burn, and Candle, Rust is quickly becoming a practical and efficient tool for serious deep learning practitioners.

Problems

4.1 Loop Benchmarking: Write a Rust program that sums the numbers from 1 to 100 million using a simple for loop. Use std::time::Instant to measure execution time. Repeat the same task in Python and compare the runtime. Briefly explain why Rust's performance is better, even for such a basic task.

4.2 Parallel Matrix Multiplication: Create two random 100×100 matrices in Rust using the ndarray crate. Divide each into four 50×50 submatrices, and compute the matrix product in parallel using the rayon crate. Combine the four sub-results to form the final matrix. Time the operation and compare it to a Python version using numpy. Discuss the observed speedup.

4.3 **Variable Lifetime and Scope**: Write a Rust function that creates a large vector inside a limited scope block:

```rust
{
    let v = vec![0u8; 100_000_000];
    println!("Vector created");
}
// At this point, the memory used by `v` is released.
```

Now compare this behavior with a similar function in Python using a large list. Use memory monitoring tools (e.g., `psutil` in Python) to observe when memory is freed. Explain how Rust's scoped lifetime helps reclaim memory precisely and automatically, without relying on garbage collection.

Part II
Advancing with Rust in AI

Chapter 5
Building Blocks of Neural Networks in Rust

5.1 Introduction

Chapter 5 introduces the core building blocks of neural networks, providing an understanding of their architecture and components. The chapter walks through the process of implementing simple neural networks in Rust, offering hands-on experience for readers. It also explores Rust's growing ecosystem for AI development, focusing on libraries and tools that enhance the creation of neural networks, including `ndarray`, `autograd`, and `linfa`. This chapter lays a practical foundation for readers to implement efficient neural network models using Rust.

Chapter Goal

- **1.** To introduce the basic architecture of neural networks and their key components.
- **2.** To provide hands-on experience with implementing simple neural networks in Rust, focusing on practical examples.
- **3.** To familiarize readers with Rust's ecosystem for AI, including libraries and tools that facilitate neural network development.

5.2 Basic Neural Network Architecture

Neural networks are a class of machine learning models inspired by the structure of the human brain. They are composed of layers of interconnected neurons that process data through mathematical functions. In this section, we'll explore the essential components that make up a neural network.

5.2.1 Implementing Perceptron

In this section, we implement a single perceptron in Rust to compute the logical AND of two binary inputs x and y. A perceptron is a linear classifier that maps input features to an output using a weighted sum and an activation function. For binary logic, we typically use a step function as the activation.

The AND function returns 1 only if both inputs are 1; otherwise, it returns 0. We model this behavior using a weighted sum and a bias term (Listing 5.1).

Listing 5.1 Simple perceptron implementing AND function

```rust
fn step(x: f64) -> u8 {
    if x >= 0.0 { 1 } else { 0 }
}

fn perceptron(x: u8, y: u8) -> u8 {
    let w1 = 1.0;
    let w2 = 1.0;
    let bias = -1.5;

    let sum = (x as f64) * w1 + (y as f64) * w2 + bias;
    step(sum)
}

fn main() {
    let inputs = [(0, 0), (0, 1), (1, 0), (1, 1)];
    for (x, y) in inputs {
        let output = perceptron(x, y);
        println!("Input: ({}, {}) => AND: {}", x, y, output);
    }
}
```

Explanation

The perceptron applies a simple formula: output $= \text{step}(w_1 \cdot x + w_2 \cdot y + b)$, where w_1, w_2 are weights and b is a bias. In this example:

- If both x and y are 1, the sum is $1.0 + 1.0 - 1.5 = 0.5$, and the step function returns 1.
- In all other cases, the sum is less than 0, and the output is 0.

Why Rust Shines Here

Rust's strict type system helps prevent common programming errors, such as unintended type conversions or misuse of incompatible types. In addition, Rust's standard library implements explicit bounds checking for indexing operations, ensuring that out-of-bounds access results in a controlled panic rather than undefined behavior. This combination of compile-time and runtime safety greatly improves program reliability without sacrificing performance in optimized builds.

For example, consider the `step` function, which takes a real number as input and returns a Boolean value indicating whether it is positive:

```rust
fn step(x: f64) -> bool {
    x > 0.0
}
```

Here, the return type `bool` is more semantically appropriate than a numeric type such as u8, since the output represents a logical condition rather than a numeric value. This example illustrates Rust's emphasis on type precision and fine-grained control over data representation, ensuring that variables reflect their intended meaning while maintaining safety and efficiency.

Building on this idea, consider the implementation of a simple logical operation such as the AND function. Since both its inputs and output are binary values, the appropriate type signature is (u8, u8) -> u8. However, when performing internal calculations, Rust does not allow implicit type casting between numeric types, unlike languages such as C++ or Python. This means that when computing expressions such as `x * w1`, both operands must explicitly share the same type. If the computation is performed using floating-point arithmetic, you must manually cast the inputs from u8 to f64, for example, by writing `x as f64 * w1 as f64`.

This explicit casting requirement contributes to numerical stability and safety: Rust ensures that arithmetic operations are only performed between values of the same type, eliminating accidental mixing of integers and floating-point numbers. While the function's final result may still be returned as a u8, performing intermediate calculations in floating-point form preserves precision. Furthermore, keeping the input types as u8 prevents invalid values such as negative numbers or fractional inputs (e.g., `-1`, `0.5`), maintaining logical consistency and correctness in the model's binary operations.

5.2.2   Implementing XOR with Perceptrons

You can model basic logic gates such as AND, OR, and NOT using a single-layer perceptron. However, implementing the XOR function with just one perceptron is impossible because XOR is **not linearly separable**. This means that no straight line (or hyperplane) can divide the input space to correctly separate the classes output by the XOR function.

Recall that the XOR function is defined as follows:

x	y	$x \oplus y$
0	0	0
0	1	1
1	0	1
1	1	0

To model XOR, we need a multi-layer structure. One simple solution is to use the identity:

$$\text{XOR}(x, y) = \text{AND}(\text{OR}(x, y), \text{NOT}(\text{AND}(x, y)))$$

This means:

1. Compute OR(x, y)
2. Compute AND(x, y)
3. Compute NOT(AND(x, y))
4. Compute AND(OR(x, y), NOT(AND(x, y)))

Using this, we can wire together multiple perceptrons to form a two-layer network that computes XOR (Listing 5.2).

Listing 5.2   Multi-layer perceptron for XOR function

```rust
fn step(x: f64) -> u8 {
    if x >= 0.0 { 1 } else { 0 }
}

// Single-layer logic gates using perceptrons
fn and(x: u8, y: u8) -> u8 {
    step((x as f64) * 1.0 + (y as f64) * 1.0 - 1.5)
}
```

```rust
9
10  fn or(x: u8, y: u8) -> u8 {
11      step((x as f64) * 1.0 + (y as f64) * 1.0 - 0.5)
12  }
13
14  fn not(x: u8) -> u8 {
15      step((x as f64) * -1.0 + 0.5)
16  }
17
18  // XOR as a composition of perceptrons
19  fn xor(x: u8, y: u8) -> u8 {
20      let or_out = or(x, y);
21      let and_out = and(x, y);
22      let not_and = not(and_out);
23      and(or_out, not_and)
24  }
25
26  fn main() {
27      let inputs = [(0, 0), (0, 1), (1, 0), (1, 1)];
28      for (x, y) in inputs {
29          let output = xor(x, y);
30          println!("XOR({}, {}) = {}", x, y, output);
31      }
32  }
```

Why Rust Shines Here

Rust's strong type system and lack of implicit type casting ensures that:

- Inputs to logic gates remain binary and valid.
- Intermediate steps must be safely converted and used—avoiding silent precision bugs.
- You get low-level control with zero-cost abstractions: ideal for performance-critical inference code.

5.2.3   Forward Propagation

In the previous examples, we manually specified the values of weights (w1, w2, b) to make the perceptron behave like logical gates. However, in a real neural network, these weight values are unknown and must be determined during a process called *training*. Training is the process of optimizing the weights so they adjust themselves based on a set of (input, output) pairs, with the goal of minimizing the prediction error of the network.

To begin this process, each weight must be initialized—typically with small random values drawn from a specific distribution—and then iteratively updated using an optimization algorithm such as gradient descent. Before we dive into the training phase, let's look at how Rust can perform forward propagation, which is the process of computing the output of a neural network given an input and a set of randomly initialized weights.

Since neural networks are inherently mathematical structures operating on multidimensional data, we will use **tensors** and **matrix operations** as the core computation tools. To support this, we need access to a numerical library that can handle tensors (like `ndarray`) and a random number generator that can produce values from common distributions (e.g., uniform, normal).

Let's first see how we can generate random values from different distributions in Rust using the
rand and `rand_distr` crates:

Listing 5.3 Random number generator

```rust
use rand::thread_rng;
use rand_distr::{Normal, Distribution, Uniform};

fn main() {
    let mut rng = thread_rng();

    // Uniform distribution between -1.0 and 1.0
    let uniform = Uniform::new(-1.0, 1.0);
    let u_sample: f64 = uniform.sample(&mut rng);
    println!("Uniform sample: {}", u_sample);

    // Normal distribution with mean 0.0 and standard deviation
        1.0
    let normal = Normal::new(0.0, 1.0).unwrap();
    let n_sample: f64 = normal.sample(&mut rng);
    println!("Normal sample: {}", n_sample);
```

The rand crate is Rust's standard library for generating random numbers. It provides tools to create
random integers, floats, and even shuffle collections. It's the core crate that underpins most random
operations in Rust. The `rand_distr` crate extends rand by adding support for statistical distributions
such as Uniform distribution, Normal (Gaussian) distribution, Exponential, Bernoulli, Poisson, and
more (Listing 5.3).

This crate is essential when initializing weights in neural networks, where we often need random
numbers drawn from specific probability distributions like Normal(0, 1) The thread_rng()
function provides a fast and secure random number generator that is local to the current thread. It
avoids the overhead of global locks and is automatically seeded, making it safe and efficient for most
use cases—including simulations and AI models.

```rust
let mut rng = rand::thread_rng();
```

Once you obtain rng, you can use it to sample values from distributions like so:

```rust
let sample = distribution.sample(&mut rng);
```

This setup is ideal for initializing neural network weights with high performance and safety in
mind—true to Rust's design principles.

This demonstrates how to generate initial weights for a neural network. In the next section, we will
use these sampled values to initialize the weight matrices and implement forward propagation over
multiple layers using matrix operations.

5.2.4 Feedforward Pass for a Three-Layer Neural Network

Now we are ready to implement the forward pass of a simple three-layer neural network in Rust. In
this example, the network is designed to approximate the function $f(x_1, x_2, x_3) = \max(x_1, x_2, x_3)$.

The network has:

- An input layer with three neurons (for x_1, x_2, x_3)
- One hidden layer with a configurable number of neurons
- One output neuron producing the scalar output

Weights and biases are initialized randomly, and we use the ReLU activation function for the hidden layer, which is defined as:

$$\text{ReLU}(x) = \max(0, x)$$

Below, Listing 5.4 is the Rust implementation using the `ndarray`, `rand`, and `rand_distr` crates.

Listing 5.4 Forward pass of a three-layer neural network

```rust
use ndarray::prelude::*;
use rand::thread_rng;
use rand_distr::{Normal, Distribution};

fn relu(x: f64) -> f64 {
    x.max(0.0)
}

// Applies activation elementwise
fn relu_layer(x: Array1<f64>) -> Array1<f64> {
    x.mapv(relu)
}

fn forward_pass(x: Array1<f64>,
                w1: Array2<f64>, b1: Array1<f64>,
                w2: Array2<f64>, b2: Array1<f64>) -> f64 {
    let hidden = relu_layer(w1.dot(&x) + &b1); // Hidden layer
    let output = w2.dot(&hidden) + &b2;        // Output layer
                                               //(no activation)

    output[0]
}

fn main() {
    let input = array![0.3, 0.8, 0.5];

    let mut rng = thread_rng();
    let normal = Normal::new(0.0, 1.0).unwrap();

    // Layer 1: 4 hidden neurons, 3 inputs
    let w1 = Array::from_shape_fn((4, 3), |_| normal.sample(&
        mut rng));
    let b1 = Array::from_shape_fn(4, |_| normal.sample(&mut rng
        ));

    // Output layer: 1 neuron, 4 hidden units
```

```rust
34    let w2 = Array::from_shape_fn((1, 4), |_| normal.sample(&
          mut rng));
35    let b2 = Array::from_shape_fn(1, |_| normal.sample(&mut rng
          ));
36
37    let result = forward_pass(input, w1, b1, w2, b2);
38    println!("Predicted output: {}", result);
39  }
```

Explanation

The forward pass computes the output as follows:

1. Compute $z_1 = W_1 x + b_1$
2. Apply ReLU: $a_1 = \text{ReLU}(z_1)$
3. Compute output: $y = W_2 a_1 + b_2$

The final output is a scalar value that approximates $\max(x_1, x_2, x_3)$. Since weights are initialized randomly, the result will only be meaningful after training. However, this example illustrates how to structure and evaluate a forward pass efficiently using matrix operations in Rust.

Why Rust Shines Here

Rust's strict typing, safety guarantees, and performance-focused design ensure:

- No unintentional memory access or null pointer dereferences
- High-performance matrix computation using crates like `ndarray`
- Memory efficiency without needing garbage collection

5.2.5 *Automatic Differentiation with* `autodiff` *Crate*

In this section, we demonstrate how to use the `autodiff` crate to calculate the derivative or gradient of multivariable functions with respect to their components. The `autodiff` crate employs **forward-mode automatic differentiation**, which is especially efficient when computing gradients of vector fields with fewer inputs than outputs. We do not delve into the details of automatic differentiation here, but interested readers can explore other crates that implement reverse-mode automatic differentiation, which is typically more efficient for scalar-output functions such as those used in deep learning backpropagation.

But how does one use `autodiff`? The first step is to define the target function using Rust's lambda syntax or closures, treating inputs as differentiable types. The crate provides the type FT<f64> to represent a floating-point number with derivative tracking enabled. Then, depending on whether the function is single variable or multivariable, you can use the functions `diff` or `grad` to compute the derivative or gradient, respectively.

In Rust, Vec<T> is a growable vector (dynamic array) of elements of a generic type T. For example, Vec<i32> represents a vector of 32-bit integers.

Before proceeding, it is helpful to formally define the concept of a **dual number**. A dual number is an extension of the real numbers of the form

$$x + \varepsilon x',$$

where x is the real (or *primal*) part, x' is the *dual* part representing a derivative-like quantity, and ε is an infinitesimal element satisfying $\varepsilon^2 = 0$. Dual numbers provide a mathematical foundation for

Table 5.1 Common autodiff types in Rust

Type	Meaning
FT<f64>	A dual number: value and its derivative, both of type f64
&[FT<f64>]	A slice (fixed-size view) of dual numbers
Vec<FT<f64»	A growable vector of dual numbers
Vec<Vec<FT<f64»>	A matrix of dual numbers represented as a vector of row vectors

forward-mode automatic differentiation by encoding both the value of a function and its derivative within the same object.

The type FT<T> defines a dual number for use with the `autodiff` crate, enabling forward-mode automatic differentiation. It internally represents a pair of values of type T, i.e., <T, T>. The first value is the actual numerical value of a variable, and the second is its derivative.

As described in the `autodiff` documentation (https://docs.rs/autodiff/latest/autodiff/forward_autodiff/type.FT.html), the type is introduced as:

```
1    pub type FT<T> = F<T, T>;
```

and defined by the following structure:

```
1    struct FT<T> {
2        pub x: T,   // The value of the variable
3        pub dx: T,  // The derivative of the variable
4    }
```

Thus, a value of type FT<f64> is a *first-order dual number*, where both the value and its derivative are of type f64. Similarly, a slice &[FT<f64>] is a borrowed list (slice) of such dual numbers, and Vec<FT<f64» is a growable vector of them. Finally, Vec<Vec<FT<f64»> represents a two-dimensional vector (i.e., a matrix) of first-order dual numbers.

In the documentation, the type FT<f64> is also provided as an alias named F1, defined as:

```
1    pub type F1 = FT<f64>;
```

However, since we want to have explicit control over the types of the variables for performance and efficiency purposes, we continue to use the explicit form FT<f64> throughout this book.

As summarized in Table 5.1, the most common autodiff types include scalars, vectors, and matrices of dual numbers.

Before we move forward to the next section, let's examine how we could access the value and its derivative in the FT type. If you define a variable of type FT, you need to introduce two f64 numbers, as follows:

```
1    let y: FT<f64> = FT { x: 3.5, dx: 2.0 };
2    println!("y.x={}, y.dx={}!", y.x, y.dx);
```

This defines a dual number $y = (3.5, 2.0)$, where the first element is the value of the variable y and the second one is the value of its derivative. To access the value of the variable, we use y.x, and to get the derivative of the variable y, we use y.dx. So the output of this code is as follows:

```
y.x=3.5, y.dx=2!
```

The method `cst` creates a constant; i.e., the derivative part will be zero. We can perform mathematical operations on dual numbers (again, we don't delve into the details of how dual numbers interact with mathematical operations, but just keep in mind that the operations behave normally on the values, while the behavior on the derivative parts follows the rules of differential calculus).

Recall that if c is a constant and u is a function of one variable, then the derivative of $c \cdot u$ is equal to c times the derivative of u, i.e., $(c \cdot u)' = c \cdot u'$. So in the following code, when we multiply a constant with a variable of type dual number, it will be multiplied with both the value and the derivative:

```
1  let a = FT { x: 3.0, dx: 1.0 };
2  let b = FT::cst(5.0);
3  let c = a * b;
4
5  println!("c={:?}", c);
```

The output will be:

```
c=(15.0V, 5.0D)
```

You can create a slice (fixed-size list) of dual numbers as follows:

```
1  let z: &[FT<f64>] = &[FT { x: 1.0, dx: 0.2 }, FT { x: 3.9, dx:
       5.8 }];
2  println!("Slice of the dual numbers{:?}", z);
```

The output will be as follows:

```
Slice of the dual numbers[(1.0V, 0.2D), (3.9V, 5.8D)]
```

Or you can create a vector of dual numbers, as follows:

```
1  let duals: Vec<FT<f64>> = vec![
2      FT { x: 1.0, dx: 0.1 },
3      FT { x: 2.0, dx: 0.2 },
4      FT { x: 3.0, dx: 0.3 },
5  ];
6
7  println!("Vectors of dual numbers{:?}", duals);
```

And the output will be:

```
Vectors of dual numbers[(1.0V, 0.1D), (2.0V, 0.2D), (3.0V, 0.3D)]
```

The core concept of the `FT` type is that, in any calculation, it tracks both the variable and its derivative at the same time, capturing the derivative at each step of the computation. This capability is critical for deep learning applications.

Now we can proceed to use the autodiff functionality for calculating the derivative of single-variable or multivariable functions. In the following examples, we walk through both scalar and multivariate differentiation with `autodiff`, laying the foundation for training neural networks using gradient descent. For the scalar differentiation (functions with one input and one output), Listing 5.5, `diff` will be used to compute the differentiation.

Listing 5.5 Derivative of a single-valued function

```
1  use autodiff::*;
2
3  fn main() {
4      // Define the function f(x)=sin(x)+e^x
5      let f = |x: FT<f64>| x.sin() + x.exp();
6      // Calculate the derivative of f at 1.0
7      let df = diff(f, 1.0);
8      println!("df = {}", df);
9  }
```

When we deal with multivariable functions (functions with more than one input and one output), Listing 5.6, autodiff using grad (Table 5.2).

Listing 5.6 Gradient of a multivariable function

```
1  use autodiff::*;
2
3  fn main() {
4      // Define the multivariable function f(v0, v1)=v0*sin(v1)+
           v1^2
5      let f = |v: &[FT<f64>]| v[0] * v[1].sin() + v[1] * v[1];
6
7      // Compute gradient at x = 1.0, y = 2.0
8      let df = grad(f, &vec![1.0, 2.0]);
9
10     println!("df/dx = {}", df[0]);
11     println!("df/dy = {}", df[1]);
12 }
```

Key Concepts for Using autodiff with Multivariable Functions

Table 5.2 Usage guide for multivariable differentiation using the autodiff crate

Concept	Explanation
Input vector	Use &[FT<f64>] – a slice of tracked variables (x, y, etc.) passed into the function
Function call	Use grad(f, &[x0, x1, ..., xn]) to compute the gradient at a specific point
Output	Returns a Vec<f64> that holds partial derivatives $\partial f/\partial x_i$ for each input
Math functions	Use method syntax: e.g., x.sin(), x.exp(), x.ln(), x.sqrt() directly on FT<f64> types

5.2.6 Backpropagation Using Automatic Differentiation

Now that we've implemented forward propagation, it's time to explore backpropagation—the process of computing the gradients of the loss function with respect to all weights and biases in the network. These gradients are then used to update the parameters in order to minimize the loss.

We continue with our previous example: a neural network designed to approximate the function $f(x_1, x_2, x_3) = \max(x_1, x_2, x_3)$. To train this network, we need a dataset of input-output pairs. Let us assume we have ten such samples as follows:

$$([3, 5, 2] \rightarrow 5), \quad ([5, 7, 1] \rightarrow 7), \quad ([1, 9, 4] \rightarrow 9),$$

$$([2, 3, 6] \rightarrow 6), \quad ([4, 1, 3] \rightarrow 4), \quad ([0, 8, 2] \rightarrow 8),$$

$$([7, 2, 1] \rightarrow 7), \quad ([6, 3, 4] \rightarrow 6), \quad ([5, 0, 2] \rightarrow 5),$$

$$([2, 6, 9] \rightarrow 9)$$

To measure the performance of the network during training, we use the **mean squared error (MSE)** loss function, which was introduced in Chapter 2. Given a predicted output $\hat{y}$ and the ground truth y, the MSE is defined as:

$$\text{MSE} = \frac{1}{n} \sum_{i=1}^{n} (y_i - \hat{y}_i)^2$$

To minimize this loss function, we must compute the gradient of the loss with respect to each weight and bias in the network. This process is known as **backpropagation** (Listing 5.7).

Manually computing these gradients can be error-prone and difficult, especially as the network becomes deeper. By automatic differentiation crates such as `autodiff`, Rust can perform this step for us. In the next section, we will show how to:

1. Perform a forward pass while recording operations.
2. Compute gradients of the loss with respect to all weights.
3. Update the weights using gradient descent.

Listing 5.7 Backpropagation

```rust
use autodiff::*;

fn relu(x: FT<f64>) -> FT<f64> {
    if x.x > 0.0 {
        x
    } else {
        FT::cst(0.0)
    }
}

fn main() {
    // --- Architecture: 3 input → 4 hidden → 1 output ---
    let input_size = 3;
    let hidden_size = 4;

    // --- Initialize weights and biases with small values ---
    let mut w1 = vec![vec![0.1; input_size];
                      hidden_size]; // W1: [4 x 3]
    let mut b1 = vec![0.0; hidden_size]; // b1: [4]
    let mut w2 = vec![0.1; hidden_size]; // W2: [4]
    let mut b2 = 0.0; // b2: scalar
```

```rust
    // Training data: (x1, x2, x3) => max(x1, x2, x3)
    let data = vec![
        (vec![3.0, 5.0, 2.0], 5.0),
        (vec![5.0, 7.0, 1.0], 7.0),
        (vec![1.0, 9.0, 4.0], 9.0),
        (vec![2.0, 3.0, 6.0], 6.0),
        (vec![4.0, 1.0, 3.0], 4.0),
        (vec![0.0, 8.0, 2.0], 8.0),
        (vec![7.0, 2.0, 1.0], 7.0),
        (vec![6.0, 3.0, 4.0], 6.0),
        (vec![5.0, 0.0, 2.0], 5.0),
        (vec![2.0, 6.0, 9.0], 9.0)
    ];

    let lr = 0.001;
    let epochs = 1000;
    for epoch in 0..epochs {
        let mut total_loss = 0.0;

        for (x, target) in &data {
            // --- Define the loss function using autodiff ---
            let loss_fn = |params: &[FT<f64>]| {
                // Unpack parameters from a flat vector:
                let mut idx = 0;

                // W1: [hidden][input]
                let w1_ft: Vec<Vec<FT<f64>>> = (0..hidden_size)
                    .map(|_| {
                        (0..input_size)
                            .map(|_| {
                                let v = params[idx];
                                idx += 1;
                                v
                            })
                            .collect()
                    })
                    .collect();

                // b1: [hidden]
                let b1_ft: Vec<FT<f64>> = (0..hidden_size)
                    .map(|_| {
                        let v = params[idx];
                        idx += 1;
                        v
                    })
                    .collect();

                // W2: [hidden]
                let w2_ft: Vec<FT<f64>> = (0..hidden_size)
```

```rust
            .map(|_| {
                let v = params[idx];
                idx += 1;
                v
            })
            .collect();

        // b2: scalar
        let b2_ft = params[idx];

        // --- Forward pass ---
        // Hidden layer output: h_i = relu(w1_i · x +
        //   b1_i)
        let h: Vec<FT<f64>> = (0..hidden_size)
            .map(|i| {
                let z =
                    (0..input_size).map(|j| w1_ft[i][j]
                        * x[j]).sum::<FT<f64>>() +
                        b1_ft[i];
                relu(z)
            })
            .collect();

        // Output: y_hat = W2 · h + b2
        let y_hat = (0..hidden_size).map(|i| w2_ft[i] *
            h[i]).sum::<FT<f64>>() + b2_ft;

        // --- Loss: MSE ---
        (y_hat - *target).powi(2)
    };

    // --- Flatten parameters into single vector ---
    let mut flat_params = vec![];
    for row in &w1 {
        flat_params.extend_from_slice(row);
    }
    flat_params.extend_from_slice(&b1);
    flat_params.extend_from_slice(&w2);
    flat_params.push(b2);

    // --- Compute gradient using autodiff ---
    let grads = grad(loss_fn, &flat_params);

    // --- Compute current loss ---
    let input_ft: Vec<FT<f64>> = flat_params.iter().map
        (|&x| FT::cst(x)).collect();
    let loss = loss_fn(&input_ft);
    total_loss += loss.x;

    // --- Update parameters using gradient descent ---
```

```rust
            let mut idx = 0;
            for i in 0..hidden_size {
                for j in 0..input_size {
                    w1[i][j] -= lr * grads[idx];
                    idx += 1;
                }
            }
            for i in 0..hidden_size {
                b1[i] -= lr * grads[idx];
                idx += 1;
            }
            for i in 0..hidden_size {
                w2[i] -= lr * grads[idx];
                idx += 1;
            }
            b2 -= lr * grads[idx]; // final bias
        }

        if epoch % 20 == 0 {
            println!("Epoch {epoch}: Loss = {:.5}", total_loss)
                ;
        }
    }
    // --- After training: test a prediction ---
    let test_input = vec![0.7, 0.4, 1.0];

    // Manual forward pass for prediction
    let hidden_out: Vec<f64> = (0..hidden_size)
        .map(|i| {
            let z: f64 = (0..input_size)
                .map(|j| w1[i][j] * test_input[j])
                .sum::<f64>()
                + b1[i];
            z.max(0.0) // ReLU
        })
        .collect();

    let y_pred: f64 = hidden_out.iter().zip(&w2).map(|(h, w)| h
        * w).sum::<f64>() + b2;

    println!("\nTest input: {:?}", test_input);
    println!("Prediction (network): {:.4}", y_pred);
    println!(
        "Ground truth (max): {:.4}",
        test_input.iter().cloned().fold(f64::NEG_INFINITY, f64
            ::max)
    );
}
```

Let's explain each part of this code. In the definition of the function `relu`, you can see that, in the `if` block, the condition is `x.x > 0.0`. The reason for this syntax is that the variable `x` is of type `FT<f64>`, meaning it is a dual number. A dual number has two components: `x.x` (the value) and `x.dx` (the derivative). Since we only need the value of `x` to check the ReLU condition, we access `x.x`.

In the `else` block, the return value should be `0`, but because the output of `relu` must also be a dual number, we return a constant dual number with zero derivative, i.e., `dx = 0`:

```
1   fn relu(x: FT<f64>) -> FT<f64> {
2       if x.x > 0.0 {
3           x
4       } else {
5           FT::cst(0.0)
6       }
7   }
```

For the rest of the code, first we need to understand the architect. The architect of this simple neural network includes three layers. The input layer of size 3, the hidden layer of size 4, and the output layer of size 1, according to the following architecture:

As discussed earlier, the loss function is the Mean Squared Error (MSE), defined as:

$$\text{MSE}(y) = \frac{1}{n} \sum_{i=1}^{n} (y_i - \hat{y}_i)^2$$

Here, y denotes the second element of the tuples (`vec![x_1, x_2, x_3]`, `y`), i.e., the label of the input vectors. The network's prediction is denoted by $\hat{y}$.

Since $\hat{y}$ depends on $\mathbf{W}_2$ and $\mathbf{b}_2$, and also on h, and since h in turn depends on z, which itself is a function of $\mathbf{W}_1$ and $\mathbf{b}_1$, the loss is ultimately a function of all these parameters. That is, the loss function depends on:

$$\mathbf{W}_1, \mathbf{b}_1, \mathbf{W}_2, \mathbf{b}_2$$

To compute the gradient of the loss function with respect to these parameters, we treat all of them as a single flattened list of values. The assumption in the code is that the loss function is already written in terms of the parameter list of type `[FT<f64>]`.

Thus, we call the loss function as `loss_fn([p_1, ..., p_k])`, where $[p_1, \ldots, p_k]$ is the reordered, flattened list combining all elements of $\mathbf{W}_1, \mathbf{b}_1, \mathbf{W}_2, \mathbf{b}_2$ (Table 5.3).

In the following piece of code, the variable `idx` tracks the current index in this flat list while reconstructing the original matrices:

Table 5.3 Architect of the neural network for predicting maximum value of three numbers

Layer	Explanation
Input Layer	$\mathbf{x} = [x_1, x_2, x_3]$ type Vec<FT<f64>>, $z = \mathbf{W}_1 \cdot \mathbf{x} + \mathbf{b}_1$, where $\mathbf{W}_1$ of size 4×3 (Vec<Vec<FT<f64>>>, and $\mathbf{b}_1$ of size 4×1 (Vec<Vec<FT<f64>>>
Hidden Layer	$h = ReLU(z)$ type Vec<FT<f64>> of size 4×1.
Output Layer	$\hat{y} = \mathbf{W}_2 \cdot h + \mathbf{b}_2$ where $\mathbf{W}_2$ is of size 1×4 and $\mathbf{b}_2$ is of size 1×1, returns scalar $\hat{y}$

```
1  let loss_fn = |params: &[FT<f64>]| {
2  // Unpack parameters from a flat vector:
3  let mut idx = 0;
4  ...
```

This defines a closure that takes a flat array of autodiff values as input.

Since we need to reconstruct the weight and bias matrices from the list of parameters in the order of $\mathbf{W}_1$, $\mathbf{b}_1$, $\mathbf{W}_2$, $\mathbf{b}_2$, the following piece of code begins reconstructing $\mathbf{W}_1$ starting from idx = 0.

By looping over hidden_size (representing the number of rows) and, within each row, looping over input_size, we extract the first 12 elements from the params list and reshape them into a 4×3 matrix representing $\mathbf{W}_1$:

```
1  let w1_ft: Vec<Vec<FT<f64>>> = (0..hidden_size)
2      .map(|_| {
3          (0..input_size)
4              .map(|_| {
5                  let v = params[idx];
6                  idx += 1;
7                  v
8              })
9              .collect()
10         })
11      .collect();
12  ...
```

Now, we don't reset the index idx and continue reconstructing $\mathbf{b}_1$ as follows:

```
1  // b1: [hidden]
2  let b1_ft: Vec<FT<f64>> = (0..hidden_size)
3      .map(|_| {
4          let v = params[idx];
5          idx += 1;
6          v
7      })
8      .collect();
```

We continue this process for $\mathbf{W}_2$ and $\mathbf{b}_2$ as follows:

```
1  // W2: [hidden]
2  let w2_ft: Vec<FT<f64>> = (0..hidden_size)
3      .map(|_| {
4          let v = params[idx];
5          idx += 1;
6          v
7      })
8      .collect();
9
10 // b2: scalar
11 let b2_ft = params[idx];
```

After this step, it is the turn to do a forward pass, which is the process of feeding input into the neural network to calculate the output. Remember that $\mathbf{W_1}$ is an 4×3 matrix and $\mathbf{x}$ is a 3×1 vector, and $\mathbf{b_1}$ is a 4×1 vector. So the matrix multiplication of $\mathbf{W_1} \cdot \mathbf{x}$ is a 4×1 vector and the result of $\mathbf{W_1} \cdot \mathbf{x} + \mathbf{b_1}$ is a 4×1 vector. To implement this, we use elementwise matrix multiplication and then feed this to the ReLU function and save the result in the memory as h as follows:

```rust
// --- Forward pass ---
// Hidden layer output: h_i = relu(w1_i · x + b1_i)
let h: Vec<FT<f64>> = (0..hidden_size)
    .map(|i| {
        let z =
            (0..input_size).map(|j| w1_ft[i][j] * x[j]).sum
                ::<FT<f64>>() + b1_ft[i];
        relu(z)
    })
    .collect();
```

The output layer just computing $\hat{y}$ which by definition is $\hat{y} = \mathbf{W_2} \cdot h + \mathbf{b_2}$ and is calculated in the following piece of code:

```rust
// Output: y_hat = W2 · h + b2
let y_hat = (0..hidden_size).map(|i| w2_ft[i] * h[i]).sum::<FT<
    f64>>() + b2_ft;
```

In the final part of the body of the definition of `loss_fn`, you only need to incorporate the formula of the loss function which is $\sum_i (y_i - \hat{y}_i)^2$, i.e.,

```rust
...
    // --- Loss: MSE ---
                (y_hat - *target).powi(2)
            };
...
```

So far we defined the loss function. But to compute the gradient of the loss function with respect to the weights and biases, we need to flatten the weights and biases that have been initialized before as a list (slice) to be able to put into the grad function, i.e.,`grad(loss_fn, params)`. The following part of the code does this:

```rust
// --- Flatten parameters into single vector ---
let mut flat_params = vec![];
for row in &w1 {
    flat_params.extend_from_slice(row); //append row to
        flat_param for all row in w1
}
flat_params.extend_from_slice(&b1); //append b1 to flat_param
flat_params.extend_from_slice(&w2); //append w2 to flat_param
flat_params.push(b2); //push b2 to flat_params
```

Where `flat_params.extend_from_slice(&b1)` method Clone and append all elements of `b1` to `flat_params`.

Now we could calculate the gradient of loss function with respect to the flattened parameter `flat_params`, i.e.:

```
1  // --- Compute gradient using autodiff ---
2  let grads = grad(loss_fn, &flat_params);
```

Next, we compute the current loss as follows:

```
1  // --- Compute current loss ---
2  let input_ft: Vec<FT<f64>> = flat_params.iter().map(|&x| FT::
     cst(x)).collect();
3  let loss = loss_fn(&input_ft);
4  total_loss += loss.x;
```

Let us explain each line in this code:

- `flat_params` is a flattened list of all weights and biases (of type `Vec<f64>`).
- The expression `.iter().map(|&x| FT::cst(x))` creates a list of *constant dual numbers*, where each value has a derivative component `dx = 0.0`.
- The constructor `FT::cst(x)` builds a dual number `FT { x, dx: 0.0 }`, indicating that this value will not participate in gradient propagation.
- The `.collect()` method gathers these into a `Vec<FT<f64»`.

This produces a dual-number version of the model parameters with zero derivatives. This gives you a dual-number version of the parameters *without triggering autodiff*. In this context, "triggering autodiff" refers to assigning nonzero derivative components (`dx 0`) to one or more inputs—an operation performed internally by the `grad` function. As a result, evaluating `loss_fn(&input_ft)` here computes only the loss value numerically, without initiating derivative propagation.

```
1  let loss = loss_fn(&input_ft);
```

This calls the `loss_fn`, which expects a slice of `FT<f64>` values. Since all `dx = 0.0`, only the value of the loss is computed (no gradients are propagated).

The next step is to run the gradient descent algorithm. Recall that the process of training a neural network is to calculate the optimal weights and biases, i.e., $\mathbf{W_i}, \mathbf{b_i}$, $i = 1, 2$, such that the updated values minimize the loss function, which itself is a function of $\mathbf{W_i}, \mathbf{b_i}$, $i = 1, 2$, i.e., $loss(\mathbf{W_1}, \mathbf{b_1}, \mathbf{W_2}, \mathbf{b_2})$. Gradient descent is a mathematical method used to reach this local minimum by iteratively updating the weights and biases with some fixed step size (learning rate), according to the following formula:

$$\text{new w1} = \text{old w1} - \text{learning rate} \times \text{gradient(loss)}$$

and similarly for `b1`, `w2`, and `b2`. Keeping this in mind, the following part of the code implements this simple update step:

```
1  // --- Update parameters using gradient descent ---
2  let mut idx = 0;
3  for i in 0..hidden_size {
4      for j in 0..input_size {
5          w1[i][j] -= lr * grads[idx];
```

```
6            idx += 1;
7        }
8    }
9    for i in 0..hidden_size {
10       b1[i] -= lr * grads[idx];
11       idx += 1;
12   }
13   for i in 0..hidden_size {
14       w2[i] -= lr * grads[idx];
15       idx += 1;
16   }
17   b2 -= lr * grads[idx]; // final bias
```

Here, `lr` is the learning rate, defined as a global variable:

```
1   let lr = 0.001;
```

And this update process is repeated over multiple iterations (epochs) to achieve convergence during training:

```
1   ...
2   let epochs = 1000;
3   for epoch in 0..epochs {
4       let mut total_loss = 0.0;
5       ...
```

The rest of the code tests the prediction on some given input.

5.3   Plotting Graphs in Deep Learning with `plotters` Crate

In deep learning applications, it is often helpful to visualize what is happening under the hood. For example, plotting the loss function over time helps determine whether a model is actually learning: if the loss tends to zero, the model is converging; if it remains flat or oscillates, the learning process may be stalled or diverging.

In this section, we introduce the `plotters` crate—a pure Rust plotting library that supports multiple back ends, including PNG, SVG, and PDF for file-based rendering, as well as GUI rendering through the `plotters-canvas` extension. When using its file-based back ends, `plotters` requires no external dependencies or bindings to Python or system libraries. However, when using graphical back ends (such as interactive GUI windows), additional system dependencies may be required depending on the platform. Overall, `plotters` is a flexible and well-documented tool that integrates smoothly into Rust-based machine learning workflows for tasks such as visualizing training loss curves.

To start, after creating a new project, you need to add the following line in your Cargo.toml file:

```
1   [dependencies]
2   plotters = "0.3"
```

In the following subsection, we will show two most common use cases of `plotters` in deep learning, plotting loss function and scatter plot.

5.3.1 *Plotting Simulated Training Loss in Rust*

The following Rust program uses the `plotters` crate to simulate and visualize the training loss of a
deep learning model.

```rust
use plotters::prelude::*;
use plotters::element::PathElement;
use rand::Rng;

fn main() -> Result<(), Box<dyn std::error::Error>> {
    let mut rng = rand::thread_rng();
    let loss_values: Vec<f64> = (0..100)
        .map(|epoch| {
            let base_loss = 1.0 / (epoch as f64 + 1.0);
            base_loss + rng.gen_range(-0.01..0.01)
        })
        .collect();

    let root = BitMapBackend::new("training_loss.png", (800,
        600)).into_drawing_area();
    root.fill(&WHITE)?;

    let max_loss = loss_values.iter().cloned().fold(0./0., f64
        ::max);

    let mut chart = ChartBuilder::on(&root)
        .caption("Simulated Training Loss", ("sans-serif", 30))
        .margin(20)
        .x_label_area_size(40)
        .y_label_area_size(50)
        .build_cartesian_2d(0..100, 0.0..max_loss)?;

    chart.configure_mesh()
        .x_desc("Epoch")
        .y_desc("Loss")
        .draw()?;

    chart.draw_series(LineSeries::new(
        loss_values.iter().enumerate().map(|(x, y)| (x as i32,
            *y)),
        &BLUE,
    ))?
    .label("Loss")
    .legend(|(x, y)| PathElement::new(vec![(x, y), (x + 20, y)
        ], &BLUE));

    chart.configure_series_labels()
        .background_style(&WHITE.mix(0.8))
        .border_style(&BLACK)
        .draw()?;
```

```
42
43        println!("Loss plot saved to training_loss.png");
44        Ok(())
45   }
```

The output of this code is shown in Figure 5.1.

Here's the full annotated explanation of the code:

```
1  use plotters::prelude::*;
2  use plotters::element::PathElement;
3  use rand::Rng;
```

- `plotters::prelude::*` brings all commonly used types and traits from Plotters.
- `PathElement` is used to draw a custom legend line.
- `rand::Rng` provides tools to generate random values (used for noise).

```
1  let mut rng = rand::thread_rng();
2  let loss_values: Vec<f64> = (0..100)
3      .map(|epoch| {
4          let base_loss = 1.0 / (epoch as f64 + 1.0);
5          base_loss + rng.gen_range(-0.01..0.01)
6      })
7      .collect();
```

- This generates 100 simulated loss values, where loss decays with epochs.
- A small amount of noise is added to each value to mimic realistic training behavior.

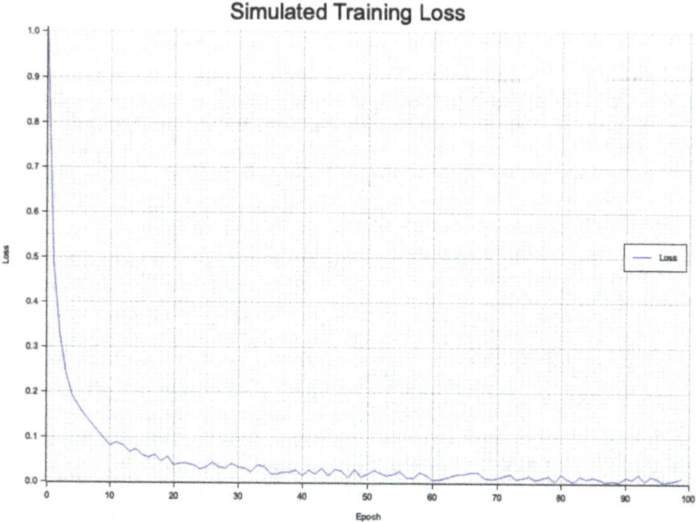

Figure 5.1 Plotting simulated training loss in Rust

```
1  let root = BitMapBackend::new("training_loss.png", (800, 600)).
      into_drawing_area();
2  root.fill(&WHITE)?;
```

- Creates a canvas with 800×600 resolution, and fills it with a white background.

```
1  let max_loss = loss_values.iter().cloned().fold(0./0., f64::max
      );
```

- Computes the maximum loss value to determine the Y-axis range.

```
1  let mut chart = ChartBuilder::on(&root)
2      .caption("Simulated Training Loss", ("sans-serif", 30))
3      .margin(20)
4      .x_label_area_size(40)
5      .y_label_area_size(50)
6      .build_cartesian_2d(0..100, 0.0..max_loss)?;
```

- Sets up the chart with title, margin, and axis ranges:
  - X-axis: 0 to 100 epochs
  - Y-axis: 0 to the max loss value

```
1  chart.configure_mesh()
2      .x_desc("Epoch")
3      .y_desc("Loss")
4      .draw()?;
```

- Adds axis labels and grid lines to the chart.

```
1  chart.draw_series(LineSeries::new(
2      loss_values.iter().enumerate().map(|(x, y)| (x as i32, *y)),
3      &BLUE,
4  ))?
5  .label("Loss")
6  .legend(|(x, y)| PathElement::new(vec![(x, y), (x + 20, y)], &
      BLUE));
```

- Draws the loss curve using a blue line.
- Adds a legend entry called "Loss".

```
1  chart.configure_series_labels()
2      .background_style(&WHITE.mix(0.8))
3      .border_style(&BLACK)
4      .draw()?;
```

- Renders the legend with a white semi-transparent background and black border.

```
1  println!("Loss plot saved to training_loss.png");
2  Ok(())
```

- Saves the final chart and informs the user.

This plot provides a simple visualization of the training process. For actual deep learning models, the loss vector would come from a real training loop. Plotters is flexible enough to work in those settings as well.

5.3.2   Scatter Plot with plotters Crate

In the classification problems or in logistic regression, it is very useful to have a visual effect on the different categories as a scattered plot with different colors. The following code shows a scattered plot of two categories with two different colors, blue and red.

```
1   use plotters::prelude::*;
2   use rand::Rng;
3
4   fn main() -> Result<(), Box<dyn std::error::Error>> {
5       let mut rng = rand::thread_rng();
6
7       // Generate 25 red and 25 blue points
8       let red_points: Vec<(f64, f64)> = (0..25)
9           .map(|_| (rng.gen_range(0.0..5.0), rng.gen_range
               (0.0..5.0)))
10          .collect();
11
12      let blue_points: Vec<(f64, f64)> = (0..25)
13          .map(|_| (rng.gen_range(5.0..10.0), rng.gen_range
               (5.0..10.0)))
14          .collect();
15
16      // Setup drawing area
17      let root = BitMapBackend::new("scatter_classified.png",
           (640, 480)).into_drawing_area();
18      root.fill(&WHITE)?;
19
20      let mut chart = ChartBuilder::on(&root)
21          .caption("Scatter Plot by Category", ("sans-serif", 30)
               )
22          .margin(20)
23          .x_label_area_size(40)
24          .y_label_area_size(40)
25          .build_cartesian_2d(0.0..10.0, 0.0..10.0)?;
26
27      chart.configure_mesh()
28          .x_desc("X")
29          .y_desc("Y")
```

```
30        .draw()?;
31
32        // Draw red points
33        chart.draw_series(
34            red_points.iter().map(|(x, y)| Circle::new((*x, *y), 4,
                  RED.filled())),
35        )?.label("Red Class").legend(|(x, y)| Circle::new((x, y),
              4, RED.filled()));
36
37        // Draw blue points
38        chart.draw_series(
39            blue_points.iter().map(|(x, y)| Circle::new((*x, *y),
                  4, BLUE.filled())),
40        )?.label("Blue Class").legend(|(x, y)| Circle::new((x, y),
              4, BLUE.filled()));
41
42        // Draw legend
43        chart.configure_series_labels()
44            .border_style(&BLACK)
45            .background_style(&WHITE.mix(0.8))
46            .draw()?;
47
48        println!("Scatter plot saved to scatter_classified.png");
49        Ok(())
50    }
```

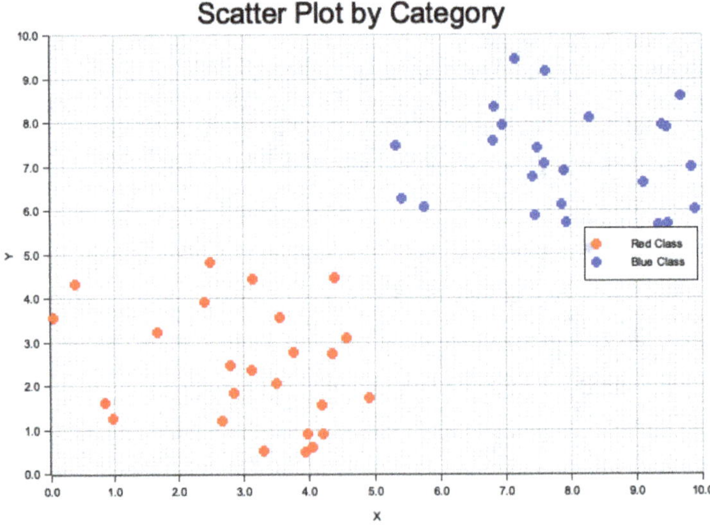

Figure 5.2 Plotting simulated scattered plot in Rust

The output of this code is shown in Figure 5.2.

In this example, we differentiate two categories of points (e.g., red vs. blue) and display them with distinct colors on a single scatter plot. Below are the newly introduced parts of the code.

```rust
// Generate 25 red and 25 blue points
let red_points: Vec<(f64, f64)> = (0..25)
    .map(|_| (rng.gen_range(0.0..5.0), rng.gen_range(0.0..5.0))
    )
    .collect();

let blue_points: Vec<(f64, f64)> = (0..25)
    .map(|_| (rng.gen_range(5.0..10.0), rng.gen_range
    (5.0..10.0)))
    .collect();
```

- This generates two distinct clusters:

  - red_points: clustered around the lower left (0–5 range)
  - blue_points: clustered around the upper right (5–10 range)

- Each point is a tuple (x, y) representing 2D coordinates.

```rust
chart.draw_series(
    red_points.iter().map(|(x, y)| Circle::new((*x, *y), 4, RED
        .filled())),
)? .label("Red Class")
    .legend(|(x, y)| Circle::new((x, y), 4, RED.filled()));
```

- This draws red circles on the chart.
- label("Red Class") assigns a name to this category for the legend.
- legend(...) defines how the category will appear in the legend.
- The same applies to the blue class drawn afterward.

```rust
chart.configure_series_labels()
    .border_style(&BLACK)
    .background_style(&WHITE.mix(0.8))
    .draw()?;
```

- This renders the chart legend box with a white semi-transparent background and black border.
- Automatically includes all labeled series.

These additions allow you to visualize classification boundaries, clustering, or labeling in a meaningful way by color-coding the categories.

Summary

This chapter provided a foundational understanding of how to implement a simple neural network from scratch in Rust. We introduced the autodiff crate, a library that supports forward-mode automatic differentiation, and demonstrated how it can be used to compute gradients and perform gradient descent training.

Although reverse-mode automatic differentiation is generally more efficient for computing gradients in deep learning applications—particularly when training large neural networks with many parameters—our focus in this chapter is primarily educational. The examples are intentionally simplified to illustrate the key ideas behind differentiable programming and automatic differentiation in Rust, rather than to achieve optimal performance. Readers should view these implementations as conceptual demonstrations of how differentiation and learning can be expressed safely and transparently within Rust's type and ownership system. Those interested in building production-grade models can explore reverse-mode autodiff crates and deep learning frameworks in the Rust ecosystem that extend these foundational concepts.

Finally, we introduced the `plotters` crate, one of the most popular Rust libraries for visualization. We showed how to use it to generate training loss curves and scatter plots, making it a useful companion for debugging and illustrating learning behavior in neural networks.

Together, these tools provide a lightweight but powerful framework for learning and experimenting with deep learning in Rust.

Problems

5.1 Dual Number Evaluation: Define a variable of type FT<f64> using:

```
1   let x: FT<f64> = FT { x: 2.5, dx: 1.0 };
```

Then compute the function $f(x) = 3x^2 + 2x + 1$ and print both the value and the derivative.

5.2 MSE Loss Gradient: Using the `autodiff` crate, compute the gradient of the loss function:

$$\text{MSE}(y, \hat{y}) = (y - \hat{y})^2$$

with respect to `y_hat`, at `y = 3.0`, `y_hat = 2.0`. Print both the loss and the gradient.

5.3 Mini Neural Net Forward Pass: Define weights $w_1 = 0.3$, $w_2 = 0.6$, and bias $b = 0.1$. For inputs `x_1 = 2.0` and `x_2 = -1.0`, compute the output of the neuron using:

$$z = w_1 x_1 + w_2 x_2 + b, \quad y = \text{ReLU}(z)$$

Use `autodiff` to compute the gradient of the output with respect to `x_1`.

5.4 Plotting ReLU Function: Use the `plotters` crate to plot the ReLU activation function:

$$\text{ReLU}(x) = \max(0, x)$$

for values of x in the range $[-5, 5]$ with an interval of 0.1. Save the output as an image file.

Chapter 6
Rust Concurrency in AI

6.1 Introduction

Modern AI systems, especially deep learning models, often perform multiple tasks simultaneously—data loading, preprocessing, training, evaluation, and logging. Efficiently managing these operations requires a clear understanding of **concurrency** and **parallelism**.

Concurrency allows different tasks to make progress independently, while parallelism executes multiple computations at the same time. Both are essential for building scalable and high-performance deep learning pipelines.

Rust provides a safe and efficient foundation for concurrent and parallel programming. Its ownership model, memory safety guarantees, and zero-cost abstractions enable developers to write reliable multi-threaded code without risking data races or memory corruption.

In this chapter, we explore how Rust's concurrency features—such as threads, channels, and synchronization primitives—can be applied to deep learning workflows, from concurrent data loading to layer-wise computation and model evaluation.

6.2 Concurrency vs. Parallelism

Modern computer architectures use multiple cores in personal computers and large GPUs to enable parallel computation. This is where the concept of concurrency becomes important. When you run a program on your computer, it gets compiled into machine code and sent to the CPU (or GPU) for execution. If you have a single-core CPU, your program will run sequentially, one instruction at a time, as the CPU receives them. But if your CPU has multiple independent processing units (cores), then your program can be split and distributed across these cores for simultaneous execution.

When different parts of a program run independently on the same processing unit and share computation time, we call it concurrent programming. On the other hand, when different parts of a program run simultaneously on separate processing units, we call it parallel programming.

In concurrency, there is typically a shared computational resource. In Figure 6.1, A_2 and B_1 share resources—A_2 produces something that B_1 consumes. In contrast, parallel computation involves no shared resources between tasks, allowing them to run fully independently, as shown in Figure 6.1.

Independent parts of a program that can run simultaneously are called **threads**. By splitting tasks across independent threads, computation can efficiently utilize available resources to perform multiple tasks both concurrently and in parallel. However, these programming models also introduce their own challenges—especially when threads access shared resources without proper coordination. Issues such

M. Maleki, *Deep Learning with Rust*, https://doi.org/10.1007/979-8-8688-2208-7_6

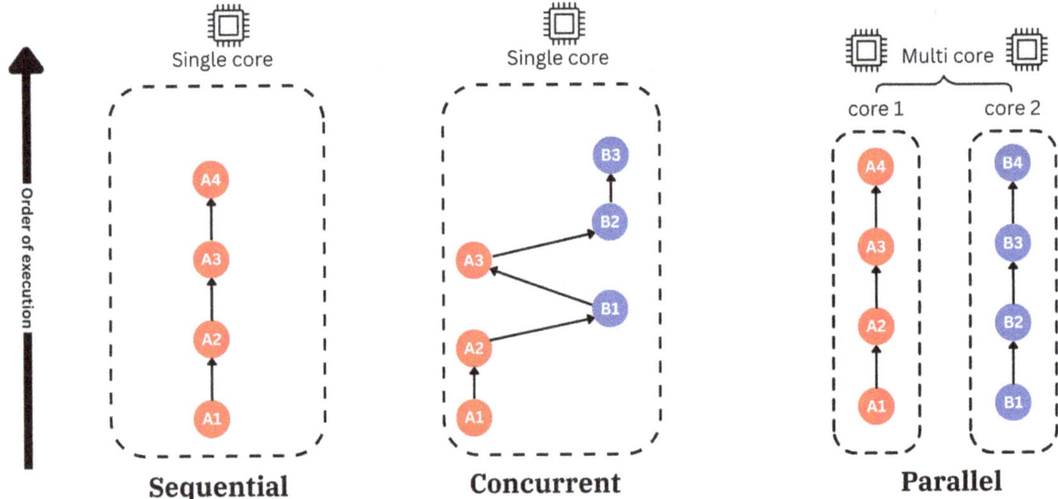

Figure 6.1 Difference between sequential, concurrent, and parallel computation

Figure 6.2 Deadlock

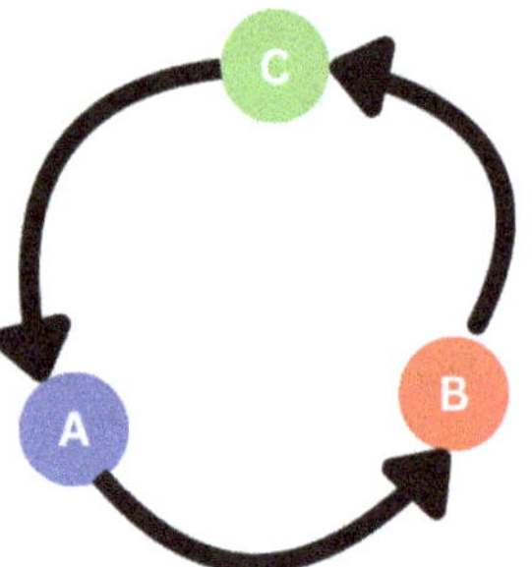

as race conditions, deadlocks, and starvation can arise in both concurrent and parallel systems, though they tend to be more severe in truly parallel execution, where multiple threads operate on different cores at the same time. We discuss these challenges in more detail below.

1. **Race Condition:** A race condition occurs when multiple threads access a shared resource without a defined order of execution. This leads to unpredictable behavior, as the final outcome depends on the timing of the thread executions. Unlike sequential or parallel computing, where execution order is well-defined, concurrency can introduce subtle bugs. For instance, if several threads access and modify shared data without synchronization, it may result in data corruption. This is especially critical in AI applications, which rely on high-quality data. Furthermore, race conditions are notoriously difficult to debug, because each individual component might behave correctly in isolation, yet the overall system fails due to nondeterministic execution order—a serious challenge in AI systems where concurrency is common.

2. **Deadlocks and Starvation:** Another major challenge in concurrent programming is managing deadlocks. A deadlock occurs when threads wait indefinitely for each other to release resources. For example, consider a scenario with three threads A, B, and C: thread A produces a resource that B consumes, B produces a resource that C consumes, and C produces a resource that A needs. If all threads wait for the others to release resources, none of them proceed, causing a deadlock (illustrated in Figure 6.2). Starvation, on the other hand, refers to a scenario where a thread is perpetually blocked from accessing a needed resource while others continue to execute, resulting in unfair resource allocation and reduced performance.

6.3   Threads and Spawn in Rust

To understand concurrency in Rust, we first need to know how to create and manage threads. Rust provides a powerful yet safe threading model through its standard library. To create a new thread, we use `std::thread` and call the `thread::spawn` function. This function takes a closure, which defines the task to run in the new thread.

In the following code, we introduce a new thread by assigning the result of `thread::spawn` to a variable called `handle`:

```rust
use std::thread;

fn main() {
    // Start a new thread
    let _handle = thread::spawn(|| {
        for i in 1..5 {
            println!("Hello from the spawned thread {}", i);
        }
    });

    // NOT waiting for the spawned thread
    // handle.join().unwrap();

    for i in 1..5 {
        println!("Hello from the main thread {}", i);
    }
}
```

The output possibly be like this:

```
Hello from the main thread 1
Hello from the main thread 2
Hello from the main thread 3
Hello from the main thread 4
Hello from the spawned thread 1
Hello from the spawned thread 2
Hello from the spawned thread 3
```

The reason for this behavior is that when the `main` function finishes execution, all the spawned threads are automatically shut down. It's as if the main thread runs to completion before the spawned threads get a chance to execute. This happens because the loop in the main thread is so fast that the operating system doesn't get an opportunity to switch context and allow other threads to run. To simulate thread switching and give spawned threads a chance to execute, we need to introduce a time delay (or sleep) in the code.

```rust
use std::thread;
use std::time::Duration;

fn main() {
    // Start a new thread
    let _handle = thread::spawn(|| {
```

```rust
 7        for i in 1..5 {
 8            println!("Hello from the spawned thread {}", i);
 9            thread::sleep(Duration::from_millis(1));
10        }
11    });
12
13    for i in 1..5 {
14        println!("Hello from the main thread {}", i);
15        thread::sleep(Duration::from_millis(1));
16    }
17 }
```

This code includes a 1 millisecond sleep, allowing the other thread enough time to execute. The output will be as follows:

```
Hello from the main thread 1
Hello from the spawned thread 1
Hello from the main thread 2
Hello from the spawned thread 2
Hello from the spawned thread 3
Hello from the main thread 3
Hello from the spawned thread 4
Hello from the main thread 4
```

When you introduce a variable but do not use it in your Rust program, the compiler will issue a warning. To suppress this warning, you can prefix the variable name with an underscore. For example, in the code above, we define the variable `handle` but do not use it. This will produce a warning. However, if we instead name it `_handle`, the warning will not appear.

If you want to have more control over the execution of threads and ensure that the spawned thread completes before the main thread continues, you can use `handle.join().unwrap();` immediately after spawning the thread, like this:

```rust
 1 use std::thread;
 2 use std::time::Duration;
 3
 4 fn main() {
 5     // Start a new thread
 6     let _handle = thread::spawn(|| {
 7         for i in 1..5 {
 8             println!("Hello from the spawned thread {}", i);
 9             thread::sleep(Duration::from_millis(1));
10         }
11     });
12     // Wait for the spawned thread to finish
13     handle.join().unwrap();
14
15     for i in 1..5 {
16         println!("Hello from the main thread {}", i);
17         thread::sleep(Duration::from_millis(1));
18     }
19 }
```

The output will be like this:

```
Hello from the spawned thread 1
Hello from the spawned thread 2
Hello from the spawned thread 3
Hello from the spawned thread 4
Hello from the main thread 1
Hello from the main thread 2
Hello from the main thread 3
Hello from the main thread 4
```

6.4   Concurrency in Deep Learning Applications

Deep learning systems—especially at scale—are not only computation heavy but also architecturally complex. Multiple stages often need to run simultaneously, such as data loading, preprocessing, model training, evaluation, and logging. Concurrency enables these stages to execute efficiently in parallel, minimizing idle time on CPUs or GPUs.

Rust's concurrency features provide a safe and performant way to implement such pipelines. In this section, we explore how concurrency is applied in deep learning, using examples that map to Rust primitives like threads, channels, and synchronization tools.

6.4.1   Concurrent Data Loading and Preprocessing

During training, deep learning models consume data in batches. To avoid delays caused by I/O operations, it is common practice to load and preprocess the next batch of data in the background, while the current batch is being used for training.

Rust Pattern   Use `std::thread` with `mpsc::channel` to establish communication between the data loader and the model trainer.

Listing 6.1   Parallel data loading with channels

```rust
use std::sync::mpsc;
use std::thread;

fn main() {
    let (tx, rx) = mpsc::channel();

    // Data loader thread
    thread::spawn(move || {
        for i in 0..5 {
            let data_batch = format!("batch {}", i);
            tx.send(data_batch).unwrap();
        }
    });

    // Training loop
```

```
16        for received in rx {
17            println!("Training on {}", received);
18        }
19    }
```

The output will be like this:

```
Training on batch 0
Training on batch 1
Training on batch 2
Training on batch 3
Training on batch 4
```

- `let (tx, rx) = mpsc::channel();` creates a channel with a transmitter (`tx`) and a receiver (`rx`). The `mpsc` module stands for *multiple producer, single consumer*, which is ideal for sending data between threads.
- A new thread is spawned using `thread::spawn`. Inside this thread, a loop sends five data batches to the main thread using `tx.send(data_batch)`. The use of `unwrap()` ensures the program will panic if sending fails—useful during development for debugging.
- The main thread runs the training loop by iterating over the receiver `rx`. The `for received in rx` syntax blocks until a message is received and ends once the sender is dropped (i.e., the data loader thread finishes).
- This pattern ensures that the training logic starts only after a batch is available, simulating real-world scenarios where data loading and training happen in parallel, without needing locks or shared memory access.

Takeaway This example showcases how Rust enables safe concurrency with zero-cost abstractions. The producer-consumer model used here is foundational in deep learning pipelines—from loading large image datasets to feeding real-time sensor data to models in production.

6.4.2 Parallelizing Computation Across Layers

In multi-threaded environments, deep learning computations can be parallelized not only across mini-batches but also across layers, especially when those layers are independent or only loosely coupled. This approach is common in custom architectures like ensemble models or in forward-pass pipelines where each layer can begin execution as soon as its input is available.

Rust Pattern Use `thread::spawn` for each layer and synchronize using `Arc<Barrier>` to ensure layers wait for each other when needed.

Listing 6.2 Layer-wise computation with thread spawning and Barrier synchronization

```
1  use std::sync::{Arc, Barrier};
2  use std::thread;
3
4  fn compute_layer(name: &str, barrier: Arc<Barrier>) {
5      println!("Computing layer: {}", name);
6      // simulate computation time
7      std::thread::sleep(std::time::Duration::from_millis(100));
```

```rust
 8        println!("Layer {} done.", name);
 9        barrier.wait(); // wait for other layers
10    }
11
12    fn main() {
13        let barrier = Arc::new(Barrier::new(3)); // synchronize 3
               threads
14
15        let b1 = barrier.clone();
16        let t1 = thread::spawn(move || {
17            compute_layer("Layer 1", b1);
18        });
19
20        let b2 = barrier.clone();
21        let t2 = thread::spawn(move || {
22            compute_layer("Layer 2", b2);
23        });
24
25        let b3 = barrier.clone();
26        let t3 = thread::spawn(move || {
27            compute_layer("Layer 3", b3);
28        });
29
30        t1.join().unwrap();
31        t2.join().unwrap();
32        t3.join().unwrap();
33
34        println!("All layers completed.");
35    }
```

The output will be as follows:

```
Computing layer: Layer 1
Computing layer: Layer 3
Computing layer: Layer 2
Layer Layer 1 done.
Layer Layer 2 done.
Layer Layer 3 done.
All layers completed.
```

Explanation

- Each `thread::spawn` runs the `compute_layer` function independently.
- The `Arc<Barrier>` is used to synchronize the threads so they all reach a certain point before continuing—similar to how stages in a deep learning pipeline must synchronize before passing data forward.
- This is a simplified version of how layer-wise forward passes can be computed concurrently and then synchronized before the next operation begins.

Takeaway Rust's threading model and synchronization primitives offer a safe, low-overhead way to parallelize layer-wise computations. This is especially beneficial when working on large models or custom pipelines that require concurrent execution of independent components.

6.4.3   *Model Evaluation During Training*

Sometimes we want to evaluate the model on validation data concurrently with training (e.g., every *N* steps), without fully pausing the main training loop. In practice, this usually requires careful coordination between threads to prevent blocking the training process.

Rust Pattern   Spawn a separate thread that periodically runs evaluation using a shared model state protected by Arc<Mutex<Model>>. While a Mutex ensures safe, exclusive access to the model during evaluation, it also temporarily blocks the training thread while the lock is held. In real systems, this can be mitigated by cloning or snapshotting the model parameters before evaluation or by using more advanced synchronization primitives such as RwLock for concurrent reads and exclusive writes.

Listing 6.3   Concurrent evaluation

```rust
use std::sync::{Arc, Mutex};
use std::thread;
use std::time::Duration;

struct Model { epoch: u32 }

fn main() {
    let model = Arc::new(Mutex::new(Model { epoch: 0 }));

    let model_clone = Arc::clone(&model);
    thread::spawn(move || {
        loop {
            thread::sleep(Duration::from_secs(5));
            let m = model_clone.lock().unwrap();
            println!("Evaluating at epoch {}", m.epoch);
        }
    });

    for epoch in 1..=10 {
        {
            let mut m = model.lock().unwrap();
            m.epoch = epoch;
        }
        println!("Training epoch {}", epoch);
        thread::sleep(Duration::from_secs(2));
    }
}
```

The output will be as follows:

```
Training epoch 1
Training epoch 2
Training epoch 3
Evaluating at epoch 3
Training epoch 4
Training epoch 5
Evaluating at epoch 5
```

```
Training epoch 6
Training epoch 7
Training epoch 8
Evaluating at epoch 8
Training epoch 9
Training epoch 10
Evaluating at epoch 10
```

6.4.4 Logging and Monitoring

Instead of blocking the training loop to write logs, we can push metrics to a logging thread through a channel.

Listing 6.4 Concurrent logging

```rust
use std::sync::mpsc;
use std::thread;

let (log_tx, log_rx) = mpsc::channel();

thread::spawn(move || {
    for message in log_rx {
        println!("[LOG] {}", message);
    }
});

log_tx.send("Epoch 1: Loss = 0.25".to_string()).unwrap();
```

Summary

Concurrency is essential in AI systems for performance and modularity. Rust provides a clean, safe, and efficient toolbox—from threads and channels to synchronization—that fits naturally with deep learning workflows. Whether it's background data loading or real-time inference, concurrency enables smarter, faster AI pipelines.

Problems

6.1 Concurrent Data Loading with Channel: Simulate concurrent data loading and training using two threads in Rust:

1. Use one thread to continuously generate and send data batches through a channel. Introduce a delay in each batch generation using `thread::sleep` to simulate I/O latency.
2. Use another thread (or the main thread) to receive and print each batch with a simulated training delay.
3. Measure the total time of execution and compare it with a purely sequential version (no concurrency).

6.2 Layer Synchronization with Barrier: Write a program that simulates the parallel execution of four layers in a neural network using `thread::spawn`.

- Each thread should represent a layer and print when its computation starts and ends.
- Use `Barrier` to ensure that all layers complete before moving to the next phase.
- Simulate varied layer execution times with `sleep`.

Explain how barriers help avoid premature transitions in a concurrent pipeline.

Chapter 7
Deep Neural Networks and Advanced Architectures

7.1 Introduction

This chapter introduces the design and implementation of deep neural networks (DNNs) in Rust, focusing on practical approaches for building and training architectures like CNNs, RNNs, and LSTMs. We explore how Rust's tools and libraries can be leveraged to construct efficient and scalable deep learning models. Through concrete examples, readers will gain insights into how to utilize Rust to create advanced neural network systems while enhancing performance in deep learning tasks.

Chapter Goal

This chapter aims to guide readers through the design and implementation of deep neural networks (DNNs) using the Rust programming language. We explore how Rust's memory safety, zero-cost abstractions, and concurrency features can be leveraged to build efficient implementations of advanced architectures such as Convolutional Neural Networks (CNNs), Recurrent Neural Networks (RNNs), and Long Short-Term Memory (LSTM) networks.

Our goal is twofold: (1) to demonstrate how DNNs are structured and trained using modern Rust crates and (2) to show how the unique characteristics of Rust can improve performance and safety in deep learning workflows.

7.2 Designing and Implementing DNNs in Rust

Deep learning requires efficient handling of high-dimensional tensors, matrix multiplications, and gradient computations. While Python dominates the ecosystem, Rust provides powerful alternatives for writing performant, safe, and maintainable code at scale.

7.3 Convolutional Neural Networks (CNNs)

Convolutional Neural Networks (CNNs) are specialized neural networks designed to process data with a grid-like topology, such as images. They are particularly powerful in capturing spatial hierarchies and patterns through shared weights and local receptive fields. Although CNNs were originally developed for image processing and computer vision tasks, they have also found applications in

© Mehrdad Maleki 2026
M. Maleki, *Deep Learning with Rust*, https://doi.org/10.1007/979-8-8688-2208-7_7

time series forecasting and Bayesian learning—for instance, in Bayesian Convolutional Neural Networks [9].

Before diving into CNN architectures, we need to understand what **convolution** is and what it does. Convolution is a mathematical operation that maps one signal to another using a function called a *kernel* (or filter). The kernel is the core component of the convolution operator.

Let's illustrate this with an example. Consider the historical daily price of a stock, for example, Apple Inc. These types of time series are often very volatile, making it difficult to detect trends. One common way to smooth the data and extract underlying trends is by using a *moving average*.

Suppose we replace each day's price with the average of the prices from the previous five days. If $x(n)$ represents the price on the nth day, the five-day moving average is given by:

$$y(n) = 0.2 \cdot x(n-4) + 0.2 \cdot x(n-3) + 0.2 \cdot x(n-2) + 0.2 \cdot x(n-1) + 0.2 \cdot x(n)$$

This is an instance of the **discrete convolution** operator, which is defined as:

$$y(n) = \sum_{i=0}^{n} x(i) \cdot k(n-i)$$

In continuous terms, the convolution is defined as:

$$y(t) = \int_{0}^{t} x(\tau) \cdot k(t-\tau) \, d\tau$$

In our example:

- $x(n)$ is the input signal (the original price)
- $y(n)$ is the output signal (the smoothed price)
- $k(n) = 0.2$ for $n = 0, 1, 2, 3, 4$ is the kernel
- and $k(n) = 0$ otherwise

The convolution operation is often denoted as $(x * k)(n)$. In practice, to compute a moving average, we convolve the input signal with a probability distribution (a kernel that sums to 1).

In this case, since we're averaging over five days, the kernel is uniform:

$$k = [0.2, 0.2, 0.2, 0.2, 0.2]$$

with $k(n) = 0$ for $n < 0$ or $n \geq 5$.

This operation is visualized in Figures 7.1 and 7.2.

The filter is not necessarily a probability distribution; it can be any function, depending on the application and the type of features we aim to extract.

The output of the convolution, denoted as $y = x * k$, is called the *feature map*, as it captures useful characteristics of the original signal through the application of the kernel.

7.3.1 CNN Building Blocks

A typical CNN consists of the following components:

- **Convolutional Layers**: Apply filters (kernels) that scan input data to produce feature maps.
- **Activation Functions**: Introduce nonlinearity (e.g., ReLU).

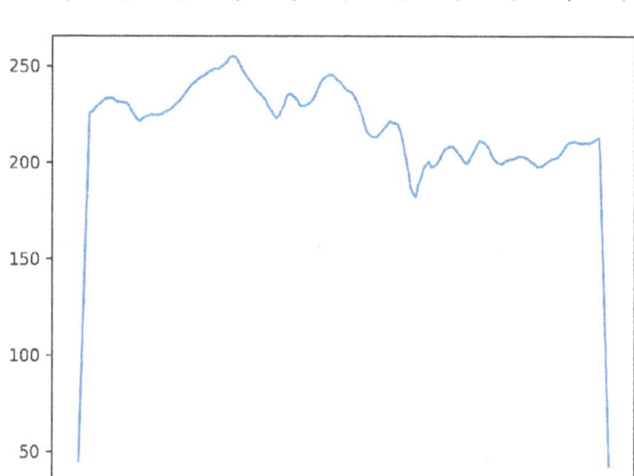

Figure 7.1 Original data of Apple Inc. daily stock price

Figure 7.2 Smoothed data using five-day moving average (i.e., convolution of x and k)

- **Pooling Layers**: Downsample feature maps to reduce spatial dimensions and overfitting.
- **Fully Connected Layers**: Classify learned features.

7.3.2   Implementing a Basic CNN in Rust

Using the `ndarray` crate, we can define basic tensor operations such as convolution and activation. A single channel image is a 2D tensor, and an image is a 3D tensor (the third one is for channel label, RGB).

Convolution vs. Cross-Correlation

Most DL libraries implement the forward "convolution" as cross-correlation:

$$S(i, j) = \sum_{m=0}^{k_h-1} \sum_{n=0}^{k_w-1} K(m, n)\, I(i + m, j + n),$$

which does *not* flip the kernel. True convolution flips the kernel:

$$S(i, j) = \sum_{m=0}^{k_h-1} \sum_{n=0}^{k_w-1} K(k_h - 1 - m, k_w - 1 - n)\, I(i + m, j + n).$$

Since $I * K = I \star K^{\dagger}$ with $K^{\dagger}(m, n) = K(k_h - 1 - m, k_w - 1 - n)$, the two differ only by a fixed flip. In CNNs with learnable kernels, this distinction is immaterial in practice, so frameworks use cross-correlation but retain the name "convolution."

Size Relationship in the Convolution Operator

Let $I \in \mathbb{R}^{H \times W}$ be a 2D input signal (e.g., an image), and let $K \in \mathbb{R}^{k_h \times k_w}$ be a 2D convolution kernel. The convolution operation (assuming no padding and unit stride) is defined as:

$$S(i, j) = \sum_{m=0}^{k_h-1} \sum_{n=0}^{k_w-1} K(m, n) \cdot I(i + m, j + n), \tag{7.1}$$

where $S(i, j)$ is defined for all $0 \le i < H - k_h + 1$ and $0 \le j < W - k_w + 1$. Therefore, the output S has shape:

$$H' = H - k_h + 1, \quad W' = W - k_w + 1.$$

This formula shows that the convolution operator reduces the spatial dimensions of the input in proportion to the size of the kernel.

Rust Implementation of 2D Convolution with Explanation

The following Rust function, Listing 7.1, performs a 2D valid convolution operation, matching the mathematical definition in Equation (7.1). It uses the `ndarray` crate for numerical array manipulation.

Listing 7.1 Valid 2D convolution in Rust using `ndarray`

```rust
use ndarray::{Array2, s};

/// Perform valid 2D convolution: output size is (H - k_h + 1,
    W - k_w + 1)
fn convolve2d(input: &Array2<f64>, kernel: &Array2<f64>) ->
    Array2<f64> {
    let (h, w) = input.dim();              // Get dimensions of the
        input matrix
    let (k_h, k_w) = kernel.dim();         // Get dimensions of the
        kernel

    let out_h = h - k_h + 1;               // Compute output height
    let out_w = w - k_w + 1;               // Compute output width

    let mut output = Array2::<f64>::zeros((out_h, out_w));  //
        Initialize output matrix

    for i in 0..out_h {
        for j in 0..out_w {
            let window = input.slice(s![i..i + k_h, j..j + k_w
                ]); // Extract a window of size k_h x k_w
            let sum = (&window * kernel).sum();
                                // Element-wise multiply and
                sum
            output[(i, j)] = sum;
                                // Store result
```

```
18                   }
19               }
20
21           output
22       }
```

Explanation

This function performs a 2D convolution of an input matrix $I \in \mathbb{R}^{H \times W}$ with a kernel matrix $K \in \mathbb{R}^{k_h \times k_w}$ using the formula:

$$S(i, j) = \sum_{m=0}^{k_h-1} \sum_{n=0}^{k_w-1} K(m, n) \cdot I(i + m, j + n)$$

The output S is a matrix of size $(H - k_h + 1) \times (W - k_w + 1)$ and contains the result of applying the kernel at each valid position of the input.

- `input.dim()` and `kernel.dim()` retrieve the shapes of the input and kernel.
- The nested loops iterate over all valid top-left positions (i, j) in the input where the kernel can be applied.
- `input.slice(...)` extracts a window of the input the same size as the kernel.
- The window and kernel are multiplied elementwise and summed using `.sum()`.
- The result is stored in the output matrix at the corresponding position.

Example

Let the input and kernel be defined as:

```
1   let input = array![
2        [1.0,  2.0,  3.0,  4.0],
3        [5.0,  6.0,  7.0,  8.0],
4        [9.0,10.0,11.0,12.0],
5        [13.0,14.0,15.0,16.0],
6   ];
7
8   let kernel = array![
9        [1.0,  0.0],
10       [0.0,-1.0],
11  ];
```

This kernel applies the operation:

$$S(i, j) = I(i, j) - I(i + 1, j + 1)$$

which measures diagonal difference.

Output

Applying the kernel at each valid location yields:

$$S = \begin{bmatrix} -5 & -5 & -5 \\ -5 & -5 & -5 \\ -5 & -5 & -5 \end{bmatrix}$$

Each output value is the result of:

$$1 \cdot I(i, j) + 0 \cdot I(i, j + 1) + 0 \cdot I(i + 1, j) + (-1) \cdot I(i + 1, j + 1)$$

which for this input always evaluates to $I(i, j) - I(i + 1, j + 1) = -5$.

Understanding `ndarray` Debug Output

When printing an `ndarray::Array2` using Rust's `Debug` trait, you may see an output like:

```
[[-5.0, -5.0, -5.0],
 [-5.0, -5.0, -5.0],
 [-5.0, -5.0, -5.0]],
shape=[3, 3], strides=[3, 1], layout=Cc (0x5), const ndim=2
```

Each part of this output describes how the array is structured in memory.

Shape (`shape=[3, 3]`)
This indicates that the array has three rows and three columns:

$$S \in \mathbb{R}^{3 \times 3}$$

Strides (`strides=[3, 1]`)
Strides determine how many steps in memory are needed to move along each axis:

- `strides[0]` = 3: To move to the next row, jump three memory positions.
- `strides[1]` = 1: To move to the next column, move one memory step.

This is consistent with C-style row-major memory layout.

Row-Major Memory Layout Example
A 3×3 array stored in contiguous row-major order would be laid out in memory as:

Memory Index:	0	1	2	3	4	5	6	7	8
Element:	S_{00}	S_{01}	S_{02}	S_{10}	S_{11}	S_{12}	S_{20}	S_{21}	S_{22}

So:

- Row 0 = indices 0 to 2
- Row 1 = indices 3 to 5
- Row 2 = indices 6 to 8

Layout Flags (`layout=Cc (0x5)`)
The `layout` field describes both the indexing order and memory contiguity:

- C – C-style (row-major) layout: last axis varies fastest.
- F – Fortran-style (column-major) layout: first axis varies fastest.
- c – Memory is contiguous in C order.
- f – Memory is contiguous in Fortran order.

These flags may appear in combinations:

Flag combination	Meaning
Cc	C-style row-major layout, contiguous in memory
Cf	C-style layout, not contiguous in memory
Ff	Fortran-style column-major layout, contiguous in memory
Fc	Fortran-style layout, not contiguous in memory

The hexadecimal code (e.g., `0x5`) is an internal bitmask used by `ndarray` for debug purposes.

Const Dimensionality (`const ndim=2`)

This indicates the number of dimensions is known at compile time (e.g., `Array2<T>`). If the dimensionality were dynamic (e.g., `ArrayD<T>`), this would appear as `ndim=2` without the `const` keyword.

Summary of Debug Fields

Field	Meaning
`shape=[3,3]`	Matrix with 3 rows and 3 columns
`strides=[3,1]`	Move 3 memory units to access next row, 1 unit to access next column
`layout=Cc`	C-style row-major layout, contiguous in memory
`const ndim=2`	Array has 2 dimensions, known at compile time

But the kernel in a CNN is not pre-engineered; it is learned during the training process. Before we dive into the learning process, let's review other key components of a CNN.

We have already discussed the concept of the **activation function**, which introduces nonlinearity into the model. Now, let's move on to the concept of **pooling**.

After the convolution layer produces a set of *feature maps* (its outputs), these maps are typically passed through a nonlinear activation function, such as ReLU. However, after this step, the model may still be sensitive to small variations in the input. To reduce this sensitivity, we feed the activated feature maps into a **pooling layer**.

The pooling layer is designed to replace a rectangular region (e.g., in a 2D image) with a *summary statistic* of that region:

- **Max Pooling**: Replaces a $p_h \times p_w$ region with the maximum value within that region.
- **Average Pooling**: Replaces it with the average value.

Pooling reduces the spatial dimensions of the feature maps. It is important to note the fundamental difference between pooling and a convolutional layer:

- In a convolutional layer, the kernel weights are learned during training.
- In pooling, the shape of the pooling region (e.g., 2×2) and the pooling method (max, average, etc.) are predefined and fixed.

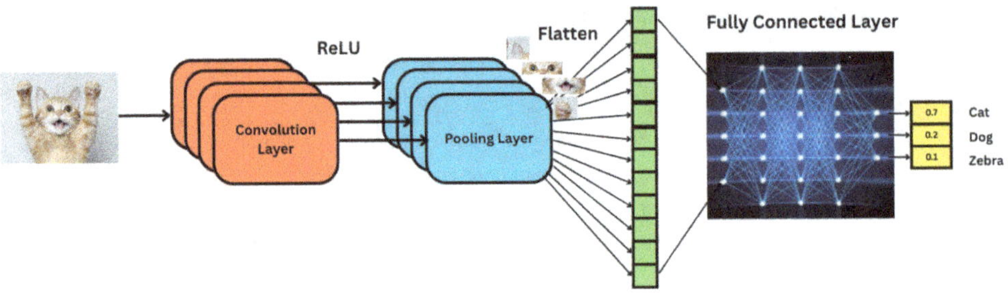

Figure 7.3 Architect of CNN

Pooling is primarily used to address **translation invariance**, meaning the network's recognition of an object is less affected by small translations or shifts in the input image.

Finally, the output from the last pooling (or convolution) stage is typically passed to a **fully connected layer**, which summarizes the extracted features into the final output. Figure 7.3 shows the architect of a single block of a convolutional neural network.

7.4 Building a CNN From Scratch in Rust

In this section, we will build a minimal convolutional neural network (CNN) from scratch without any deep learning libraries. We will use only the Rust standard library and implement the forward and backward passes ourselves.

The complete CNN will consist of:

1. Convolution layer
2. ReLU activation
3. Max pooling
4. Fully connected (FC) layer
5. Sigmoid activation
6. Binary cross-entropy loss
7. Stochastic gradient descent (SGD) updates

We will construct the CNN incrementally in small building blocks.

7.4.1 Step 1: Activation Functions

We begin by defining the activation functions and their derivatives.

```rust
fn sigmoid(x: f32) -> f32 {
    1.0 / (1.0 + (-x).exp())
}

fn relu(x: f32) -> f32 {
    if x > 0.0 { x } else { 0.0 }
}
```

```rust
 8
 9  fn relu_deriv(x: f32) -> f32 {
10      if x > 0.0 { 1.0 } else { 0.0 }
11  }
```

Explanation

- `sigmoid`: Maps any real number to the range (0, 1), suitable for probability outputs.
- `relu`: Keeps positive inputs and sets negative inputs to zero, introducing nonlinearity.
- `relu_deriv`: Derivative of ReLU, needed during backpropagation.

7.4.2   Step 2: Loss Function

We use binary cross-entropy for binary classification.

```rust
1  fn binary_cross_entropy(y_true: f32, y_pred: f32) -> f32 {
2      -(y_true * y_pred.ln() + (1.0 - y_true) * (1.0 - y_pred).ln
         ())
3  }
```

Explanation

- Measures the error between predicted probability `y_pred` and true label `y_true`.
- Large penalty for confident but wrong predictions.

7.4.3   Step 3: Convolution Operation

We implement a simple 2D convolution for grayscale images.

```rust
 1  fn conv2d(input: &Vec<Vec<f32>>, kernel: &Vec<Vec<f32>>) -> Vec
      <Vec<f32>> {
 2      let h = input.len();
 3      let w = input[0].len();
 4      let kh = kernel.len();
 5      let kw = kernel[0].len();
 6      let mut output = vec![vec![0.0; w - kw + 1]; h - kh + 1];
 7
 8      for i in 0..(h - kh + 1) {
 9          for j in 0..(w - kw + 1) {
10              let mut sum = 0.0;
11              for m in 0..kh {
12                  for n in 0..kw {
13                      sum += input[i + m][j + n] * kernel[m][n];
14                  }
15              }
16              output[i][j] = sum;
```

```
17            }
18        }
19        output
20    }
```

Explanation

- `input`: 2D vector representing a grayscale image.
- `kernel`: Small filter matrix that is slid over the image.
- Produces an `output` feature map where each value is the dot product between the kernel and the image patch it covers.

7.4.4 Step 4: Convolution Backpropagation

We update kernel weights using gradients from the output.

```
1  fn conv2d_backprop(
2      d_out: &Vec<Vec<f32>>,
3      input: &Vec<Vec<f32>>,
4      kernel: &mut Vec<Vec<f32>>,
5      lr: f32,
6  ) {
7      let kh = kernel.len();
8      let kw = kernel[0].len();
9      for m in 0..kh {
10         for n in 0..kw {
11             let mut grad = 0.0;
12             for i in 0..d_out.len() {
13                 for j in 0..d_out[0].len() {
14                     grad += input[i + m][j + n] * d_out[i][j];
15                 }
16             }
17             kernel[m][n] -= lr * grad;
18         }
19     }
20 }
```

Explanation

- `d_out`: Gradient of loss with respect to convolution output.
- For each kernel weight, sum contributions from all positions where the weight was applied.
- Update each kernel weight using learning rate `lr`.

7.4.5 Step 5: Max Pooling

Pooling reduces spatial dimensions and adds translation invariance.

```rust
fn max_pool2x2(input: &Vec<Vec<f32>>) -> (Vec<Vec<f32>>, Vec<
    Vec<(usize, usize)>>) {
    let h = input.len() / 2;
    let w = input[0].len() / 2;
    let mut output = vec![vec![0.0; w]; h];
    let mut max_pos = vec![vec![(0, 0); w]; h];

    for i in 0..h {
        for j in 0..w {
            let mut max_val = f32::MIN;
            let mut pos = (0, 0);
            for m in 0..2 {
                for n in 0..2 {
                    let val = input[i * 2 + m][j * 2 + n];
                    if val > max_val {
                        max_val = val;
                        pos = (i * 2 + m, j * 2 + n);
                    }
                }
            }
            output[i][j] = max_val;
            max_pos[i][j] = pos;
        }
    }
    (output, max_pos)
}
```

Explanation

- Divides input into 2×2 blocks.
- Outputs the maximum value from each block.
- Records the position of the maximum value for use in backpropagation.

7.4.6 Step 6: Max Pooling Backpropagation

We propagate gradients only to the positions of the maximum values.

```rust
fn max_pool2x2_backprop(
    d_out: &Vec<Vec<f32>>,
    max_pos: &Vec<Vec<(usize, usize)>>,
    h: usize,
    w: usize,
) -> Vec<Vec<f32>> {
    let mut d_input = vec![vec![0.0; w]; h];
```

```
8        for i in 0..d_out.len() {
9            for j in 0..d_out[0].len() {
10               let (mi, mj) = max_pos[i][j];
11               d_input[mi][mj] = d_out[i][j];
12           }
13       }
14       d_input
15  }
```

Explanation

- Starts with zero gradients for the whole input.
- For each pooling block, places the gradient only at the position where the maximum value occurred in the forward pass.

What This CNN Does

The CNN we implemented takes an (image, label) pair as input:

- image: A 2D array of pixel intensities (in our example, grayscale values).
- label: Either 1.0 (if the image contains a cat) or 0.0 (if it does not contain a cat).

  During the forward pass:

1. The image is processed by the convolution layer to extract spatial features.
2. A ReLU activation introduces nonlinearity.
3. Max pooling reduces spatial size and keeps the most important activations.
4. The pooled features are flattened and fed into a fully connected (FC) layer.
5. A sigmoid activation at the output layer produces a probability $\hat{y}$ between 0 and 1.

  If $\hat{y}$ is close to 1.0, the model predicts "cat"; if it is close to 0.0, it predicts "not cat."

How Training Works

Training adjusts the weights of the convolution kernels and the FC layer so that the model's predictions match the labels in the dataset. The process is:

1. **Forward Pass**: Pass the input image through the network to compute the predicted probability $\hat{y}$.
2. **Loss Calculation**: Use the binary cross-entropy loss function to measure how far $\hat{y}$ is from the true label y.
3. **Backward Pass**: Compute gradients of the loss with respect to all trainable parameters using backpropagation.
4. **Parameter Update**: Adjust the weights using stochastic gradient descent (SGD) with a learning rate η:

$$w \leftarrow w - \eta \cdot \frac{\partial L}{\partial w}$$

Example: Cat vs. Non-Cat Dataset

If the training dataset consists of:

- Images of cats with label $y = 1.0$
- Images of non-cats with label $y = 0.0$

the CNN will learn to detect patterns in the pixel data that are characteristic of cats (such as fur textures, ear shapes, or eye patterns) and distinguish them from non-cat patterns.

After enough training epochs:

- Feeding a new image of a cat should give $\hat{y} \approx 1.0$.
- Feeding a non-cat image should give $\hat{y} \approx 0.0$.

7.4.7 Step 7: Training the CNN Step by Step

We now train our CNN on a small toy dataset: two 6×6 grayscale images—one labeled as "cat" ($y = 1.0$) and the other as "non-cat" ($y = 0.0$).

1. Define the Dataset

```rust
let dataset = vec![
    (cat_image_matrix, 1.0),      // Cat
    (non_cat_image_matrix, 0.0),  // Not cat
];
```

Explanation Each dataset entry is a tuple (image, label) where:

- image is a 6×6 matrix of pixel values.
- label is 1.0 for cats and 0.0 for non-cats.

2. Initialize Parameters

```rust
let mut kernel = vec![
    vec![0.1, 0.2, -0.1],
    vec![0.0, 0.1,  0.1],
    vec![-0.2, 0.0, 0.2],
];
```

Explanation The convolution kernel is initialized with small values. This kernel will be updated during training to detect features.

3. Determine Fully Connected (FC) Layer Size

```rust
let temp_conv = conv2d(&dataset[0].0, &kernel);
let (temp_pool, _) = max_pool2x2(&temp_conv);
let flat_len = temp_pool.len() * temp_pool[0].len();

let mut fc_weights = vec![0.5; flat_len];
let mut fc_bias = 0.0;
let lr = 0.01;
```

Explanation We run one forward pass to find the shape after convolution and pooling and then allocate the FC layer weights accordingly.

4. Training Loop Over Epochs

```rust
for epoch in 0..50 {
    let mut total_loss = 0.0;
```

```
3
4      for (image, label) in &dataset {
5          // Forward + Backward pass will go here
6      }
7
8      println!("Epoch {}: Loss = {:.4}", epoch, total_loss /
           dataset.len() as f32);
9  }
```

Explanation We train for 50 epochs. For each epoch, we loop over every image in the dataset.

5. Forward Pass

```
1   // Convolution + ReLU
2   let mut conv_out = conv2d(image, &kernel);
3   for i in 0..conv_out.len() {
4       for j in 0..conv_out[0].len() {
5           conv_out[i][j] = relu(conv_out[i][j]);
6       }
7   }
8
9   // Max pooling
10  let (pool_out, max_pos) = max_pool2x2(&conv_out);
11
12  // Flatten
13  let flat = flatten(&pool_out);
14
15  // Fully connected layer + sigmoid
16  let z: f32 = flat.iter()
17      .zip(fc_weights.iter())
18      .map(|(x, w)| x * w)
19      .sum::<f32>() + fc_bias;
20  let y_pred = sigmoid(z);
21
22  // Compute loss
23  let loss = binary_cross_entropy(*label, y_pred);
24  total_loss += loss;
```

Explanation The forward pass extracts features with convolution and pooling, flattens them, and feeds them to the FC layer to produce a probability y_{pred}.

6. Backward Pass

```
1   // Gradient for output
2   let dz = y_pred - label;
3
4   // Update FC weights and bias
5   for i in 0..fc_weights.len() {
6       fc_weights[i] -= lr * dz * flat[i];
7   }
```

```rust
 8    fc_bias -= lr * dz;
 9
10    // Backprop to pooled layer
11    let mut d_pool_out = vec![vec![0.0; pool_out[0].len()];
          pool_out.len()];
12    let mut idx = 0;
13    for i in 0..pool_out.len() {
14        for j in 0..pool_out[0].len() {
15            d_pool_out[i][j] = dz * fc_weights[idx];
16            idx += 1;
17        }
18    }
19
20    // Unpooling
21    let d_conv_out = max_pool2x2_backprop(
22        &d_pool_out, &max_pos,
23        conv_out.len(), conv_out[0].len()
24    );
25
26    // Backprop through ReLU
27    let mut d_conv_out_relu = vec![vec![0.0; conv_out[0].len()];
          conv_out.len()];
28    for i in 0..conv_out.len() {
29        for j in 0..conv_out[0].len() {
30            d_conv_out_relu[i][j] = d_conv_out[i][j] * relu_deriv(
                conv_out[i][j]);
31        }
32    }
33
34    // Update convolution kernel
35    conv2d_backprop(&d_conv_out_relu, image, &mut kernel, lr);
```

Explanation We compute the gradient at the output and propagate it backward through:

1. The fully connected layer
2. Max pooling (unpooling step)
3. ReLU activation
4. Convolution kernel update

This adjusts all trainable parameters to reduce the loss.

7. Final Output

```rust
1    println!("Trained kernel: {:?}", kernel);
2    println!("Trained FC weights: {:?}", fc_weights);
```

Explanation After training, the kernel and FC weights are tuned so that the network predicts values close to 1.0 for cats and 0.0 for non-cats.

7.4.8   Using the Trained CNN for Prediction

Once training is complete, the convolution kernel and fully connected (FC) layer weights contain learned patterns from the training data.

What the Parameters Represent

- **Convolution Kernel:** Detects low-level patterns in the input image (e.g., edges, textures, shapes) that are useful for distinguishing cats from non-cats.
- **FC Weights and Bias:** Combine the extracted features into a final score that indicates the probability of the image being a cat.

Making a Prediction

To classify a new image:

1. Apply the same forward pass as during training:

    a. Convolution with the *trained* kernel.
    b. ReLU activation.
    c. Max pooling.
    d. Flattening.
    e. Fully connected layer using *trained* FC weights and bias.
    f. Sigmoid activation to produce a probability $\hat{y} \in (0, 1)$.

2. If $\hat{y} \geq 0.5$, predict cat (label 1); otherwise, predict non-cat (label 0).

Example Prediction Code

```rust
fn predict(
    image: &Vec<Vec<f32>>,
    kernel: &Vec<Vec<f32>>,
    fc_weights: &Vec<f32>,
    fc_bias: f32
) -> f32 {
    let mut conv_out = conv2d(image, kernel);
    for row in conv_out.iter_mut() {
        for val in row.iter_mut() {
            *val = relu(*val);
        }
    }
    let (pool_out, _) = max_pool2x2(&conv_out);
    let flat = flatten(&pool_out);
    let z: f32 = flat.iter().zip(fc_weights.iter())
                    .map(|(x, w)| x * w)
                    .sum::<f32>() + fc_bias;
    sigmoid(z) // probability of "cat"
}
```

How to Use It

```rust
let prob = predict(&new_image, &kernel, &fc_weights, fc_bias);
if prob >= 0.5 {
    println!("Prediction: Cat ({:.2}%)", prob * 100.0);
```

```
4  } else {
5      println!("Prediction: Not Cat ({:.2}%)", prob * 100.0);
6  }
```

Key Point

We do not run backpropagation for prediction. The forward pass alone is enough once the network has learned good parameters.

7.5   Recurrent Neural Networks (RNN)

There are many real-world problems that cannot be effectively modeled using either feed-forward neural networks or convolutional neural networks (CNNs). While CNNs are powerful because of *parameter sharing*—applying the same kernel across different spatial positions—they are inherently designed for fixed-size inputs and do not retain any notion of temporal memory.

In tasks involving **sequential data**, however, the order and dependency between elements are crucial. Examples include:

- **Natural Language**: Where grammar and meaning depend on earlier words in a sentence
- **Financial Time Series**: Where future prices are influenced by historical trends
- **Speech and Audio**: Where information unfolds over time

In such cases, we need a neural network architecture that can store information from previous time steps and use it to influence current predictions. This is the motivation behind the **Recurrent Neural Network (RNN)**.

7.5.1   RNNs as Dynamical Systems

We can think of an RNN as a discrete-time dynamical system. If $\mathbf{x}(t)$ represents the input at time step t and $\mathbf{h}(t)$ is the hidden state summarizing all information from time steps 1 to t, then the network evolves according to:

$$\mathbf{h}(t) = \sigma_h \left(W_h \mathbf{h}(t-1) + W_x \mathbf{x}(t) + \mathbf{b}_h \right)$$

Here:

- $\mathbf{h}(t-1)$ carries information from the past.
- $\mathbf{x}(t)$ is the current input (e.g., the embedding of the current word).
- W_h is the recurrent weight matrix applied to the previous hidden state.
- W_x is the input weight matrix applied to the current input.
- σ_h is a nonlinear activation function such as tanh or ReLU.
- $\mathbf{b}_h$ is a bias term.

The output $\mathbf{y}(t)$ at each time step is computed from the hidden state:

$$\mathbf{y}(t) = \sigma_y \left(W_y \mathbf{h}(t) + \mathbf{b}_y \right)$$

where W_y and $\mathbf{b}_y$ are the parameters of the output layer and σ_y is typically a softmax when performing classification.

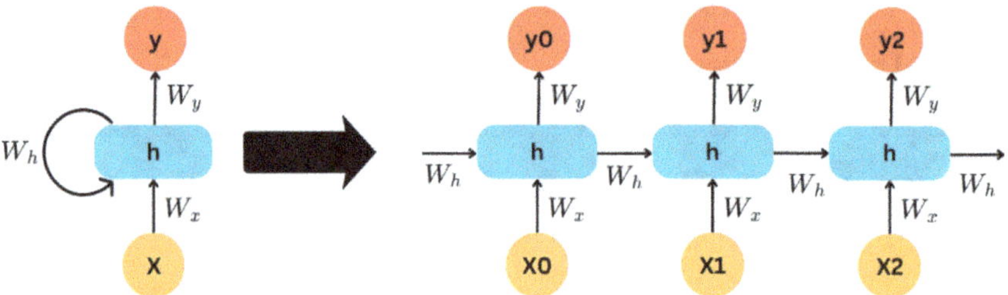

Figure 7.4 Unfolded architecture of an RNN over three time steps

Figure 7.4 shows the unfolded architecture of an RNN over three time steps. The same parameters W_h, W_x, and W_y are reused (shared) across time.

7.5.2   *Fixed-Size Input/Output RNNs*

Depending on the task, the input and output sequences may have fixed lengths. This gives rise to several configurations:

1. **One to Many**: A single input produces a sequence of outputs. For example, in *image captioning* (Figure 7.5), an image is first encoded into an initial hidden state, and then a sequence of words is generated step by step.
2. **Many to One**: A sequence of inputs produces a single output. For example, in *sentiment analysis* (Figure 7.6), the entire sequence of words in a review is processed, and the final hidden state is classified as positive or negative sentiment.
3. **Many to Many (fixed length)**: A sequence of inputs produces a sequence of outputs of the same length. For example, in *named-entity recognition* (Figure 7.7), each word in a sentence is assigned a label such as `Person`, `Organization`, or `Location`.

Figure 7.5   One to many

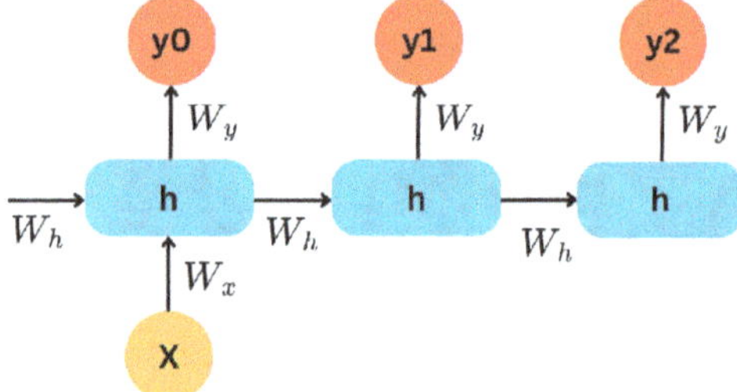

Figure 7.6   Many to one

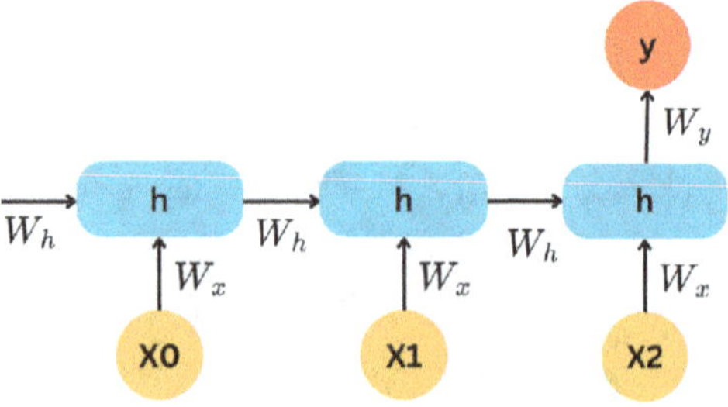

Figure 7.7 Many to many

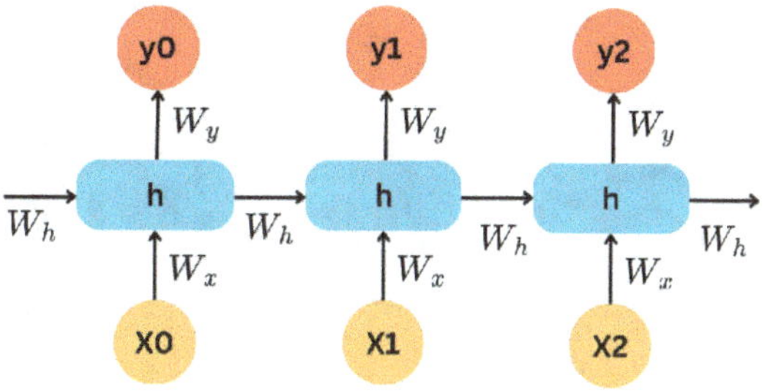

In all these cases, the recurrence formula remains the same, but the way outputs are read from the hidden states differs.

7.5.3   *Variable-Size Input/Output: Encoder-Decoder (Seq2Seq)*

When input and output sequences can have *different* lengths, the fixed-size RNN architectures are insufficient. In such cases, we use an **encoder-decoder** architecture, also known as *sequence to sequence* (Seq2Seq). This is a special case of many to many, but with variable input and output lengths.

Encoder
The encoder RNN reads the input sequence $\mathbf{x}(1), \ldots, \mathbf{x}(T_{in})$ and compresses it into a fixed-length **context vector c**, typically taken as the final hidden state of the encoder:

$$\mathbf{h}_E(t) = \sigma_h\left(W_h^E \mathbf{h}_E(t-1) + W_x^E \mathbf{x}(t) + \mathbf{b}_h^E\right), \quad \mathbf{c} = \mathbf{h}_E(T_{in})$$

Decoder
The decoder RNN generates the output sequence $\mathbf{y}(1), \ldots, \mathbf{y}(T_{out})$ one token at a time. At each step, it takes as input the previous output token and the context vector $\mathbf{c}$ (passed either directly or via initialization of $\mathbf{h}_D(0)$):

$$\mathbf{h}_D(t) = \sigma_h\left(W_h^D \mathbf{h}_D(t-1) + W_x^D \mathbf{y}(t-1) + W_c \mathbf{c} + \mathbf{b}_h^D\right)$$

$$\hat{\mathbf{y}}(t) = \sigma_y\left(W_y \mathbf{h}_D(t) + \mathbf{b}_y\right)$$

The context vector acts as a compressed representation of the entire input sequence. In Figure 7.8, the left block shows the encoder compressing the input into $\mathbf{c}$, and the right block shows the decoder expanding $\mathbf{c}$ into the output sequence.

7.5.4   *Training RNNs*

Training an RNN follows the same general principle as training other neural networks: we adjust the parameters to minimize a loss function. However, because RNNs process sequences, the training set and gradient computation are specialized.

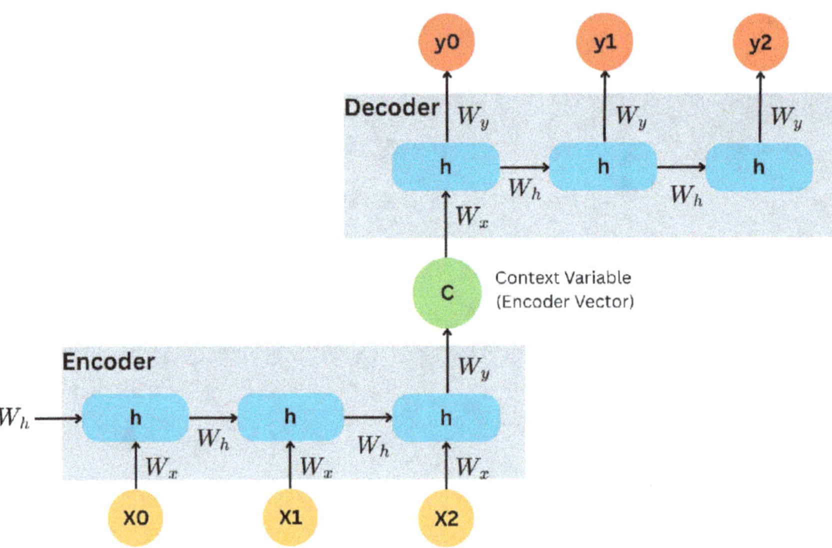

Figure 7.8 Encoder-Decoder

Training Set Structure

The structure of the training set depends on the task:

- In **many-to-one** tasks (e.g., sentiment analysis), each training example consists of a sequence of tokens $\{\mathbf{x}(1), \ldots, \mathbf{x}(T)\}$ paired with a single target label y.
- In **many-to-many** tasks with fixed length (e.g., named-entity recognition), each input token has a corresponding output token, so the dataset contains aligned pairs $\{(\mathbf{x}(t), \mathbf{y}(t))\}_{t=1}^{T}$.
- In **sequence-to-sequence** tasks (e.g., machine translation), the dataset contains pairs of sequences: $(\mathbf{x}^{(1)}, \ldots, \mathbf{x}^{(T_{in})})$ as input and $(\mathbf{y}^{(1)}, \ldots, \mathbf{y}^{(T_{out})})$ as target output.

In all cases, the RNN produces a predicted output $\hat{\mathbf{y}}(t)$ at each relevant time step, which is compared to the ground truth $\mathbf{y}(t)$ using a loss function such as cross-entropy.

Loss Computation

For example, in a classification setting with vocabulary size K, the cross-entropy loss over a sequence of length T is:

$$\mathcal{L} = -\sum_{t=1}^{T} \sum_{k=1}^{K} y_k(t) \log \hat{y}_k(t)$$

where:

- $y_k(t) \in \{0, 1\}$ is the ground truth indicator for class k at time t.
- $\hat{y}_k(t)$ is the predicted probability for class k at time t.

The goal of training is to adjust all weights W_x, W_h, W_y and biases to minimize $\mathcal{L}$ over all sequences in the training set.

Backpropagation Through Time (BPTT)

Because an RNN reuses the same parameters across all time steps, we cannot treat each step as an independent layer. Instead, we *unroll* the RNN across the sequence, as shown in Figure 7.4, and compute gradients through all time steps simultaneously.

The derivative of the loss with respect to the recurrent weights W_h involves a sum over all time steps due to the chain rule:

$$\frac{\partial \mathcal{L}}{\partial W_h} = \sum_{t=1}^{T} \frac{\partial \mathcal{L}}{\partial \mathbf{h}(t)} \cdot \frac{\partial \mathbf{h}(t)}{\partial W_h}$$

and

$$\frac{\partial \mathbf{h}(t)}{\partial W_h} = \frac{\partial \mathbf{h}(t)}{\partial \mathbf{h}(t-1)} \cdot \frac{\partial \mathbf{h}(t-1)}{\partial W_h}$$

This recursive dependency means that errors are propagated backward in time through the recurrent connections—hence the name *Backpropagation Through Time*.

Concretely:

1. Run a forward pass over the entire sequence to store all hidden states $\mathbf{h}(1), \ldots, \mathbf{h}(T)$.
2. Compute the loss $\mathcal{L}$ over the outputs.
3. Starting from $t = T$ and moving backward to $t = 1$, compute the error gradients with respect to the hidden states and parameters.
4. Update the parameters using gradient descent or its variants.

Vanishing and Exploding Gradients

Because the recurrent gradient involves repeated multiplication by the Jacobian $\frac{\partial \mathbf{h}(t)}{\partial \mathbf{h}(t-1)}$, if the spectral radius of W_h is less than 1, the gradients tend to vanish, and if greater than 1, they can explode. This instability underlies the training difficulties of plain RNNs when processing long sequences and has motivated several architectural innovations aimed at improving gradient flow. Residual connections, introduced in ResNet [4], and later extended in HeunNet [6], address this issue by drawing analogies between deep networks and numerical integration methods for differential equations. While ResNet can be viewed as a discrete approximation of Euler's method, HeunNet adopts the more accurate predictor-corrector Heun scheme, improving stability and convergence in deep architectures.

7.6   A Minimal RNN in Rust with `tch`

7.6.1   *Context and Problem Statement*

Before diving into the architecture and code, let's clarify the task this RNN is trained to solve. We want to test and demonstrate a minimal recurrent neural network's ability to *learn temporal dependencies* in a controlled, synthetic setting.

The chosen toy problem is:

Given a sequence of discrete tokens $x_1, x_2, \ldots, x_T$ from a vocabulary of size V, predict at each time step the token that is exactly one index higher (modulo V):

$$y_t = (x_t + 1) \bmod V.$$

This problem has several advantages for demonstration purposes:

1. It is **simple and fully deterministic**, so we know the optimal accuracy is 100%.
2. It requires the model to produce an *output at every time step* (many-to-many mapping).

3. It is a good test for **Backpropagation Through Time (BPTT)** because the model must learn from sequences rather than isolated samples.
4. It allows us to verify that the forward pass, the recurrent update, and gradient propagation are implemented correctly.

In practical applications, the same structure could be adapted to tasks such as:

- Language modeling (predicting the next character or word).
- Sensor time series forecasting (predicting the next measurement given history).
- Sequence tagging (POS tagging, named entity recognition, etc.).

Goal Achieve perfect accuracy on the mapping $x_t \mapsto (x_t + 1) \bmod V$ for all t in a short sequence, proving that our hand-built RNN cell and training loop in Rust are functionally correct.

In this walk-through, we keep the implementation exactly as in the core description and explain it in small, focused listings. Each listing is self-contained and directly corresponds to the math in the previous subsection.

7.6.1.1   Step 1: Batch Generator (Inputs + Labels)

We synthesize short sequences and their targets. Inputs are integer tokens; targets are the shift-by-1 version; inputs are then one-hot encoded, Listing 7.2.

Listing 7.2 Mini-batch generator: returns (x-idx, y-idx, x-onehot)

```rust
use tch::{Device, Kind, Tensor};

fn make_batch(batch: i64, t_steps: i64, vocab: i64, device:
    Device) -> (Tensor, Tensor, Tensor) {
    let x_idx = Tensor::randint(vocab, [batch, t_steps], (Kind
        ::Int64, device));
    let y_idx = (&x_idx + 1).remainder(vocab);
        // teacher: shift-by-1 (mod V)
    let x_onehot = x_idx.one_hot(vocab).to_kind(Kind::Float);
        // (B, T, V)
    (x_idx, y_idx, x_onehot)
}
```

What It Does $\texttt{x\_idx} \in \mathbb{Z}^{B \times T}$ holds token IDs; $\texttt{y\_idx} = (\texttt{x\_idx} + 1) \bmod V$ holds target IDs; $\texttt{x\_onehot} \in \mathbb{R}^{B \times T \times V}$ is the one-hot input tensor. This matches the many-to-many objective where each time step has a label.

7.6.1.2   Step 2: Model Parameters (Manual Cell)

We construct the vanilla (tanh) RNN cell explicitly from linear maps so the math is transparent (Listing 7.3):

$$\mathbf{h}_t = \tanh(\mathbf{x}_t W_x + \mathbf{h}_{t-1} W_h + \mathbf{b}_h), \qquad \mathbf{o}_t = \mathbf{h}_t W_y + \mathbf{b}_y.$$

Listing 7.3 Parameters for the RNN cell and the per-step classifier

```rust
use tch::{nn, nn::OptimizerConfig, Device, Kind, Tensor};

let device = Device::cuda_if_available();
let vs = nn::VarStore::new(device);
let root = &vs.root();

// dims / hyperparameters
let vocab:  i64 = 6;     // input & output size V
let hidden: i64 = 16;    // hidden size H
let t_steps: i64 = 8;    // sequence length T
let batch:  i64 = 32;    // batch size B
let epochs: i64 = 120;   // training epochs

// explicit cell: (V->H) + (H->H) -> tanh -> (H->V)
let wx = nn::linear(root / "wx", vocab,  hidden, Default::
    default()); // W_x
let wh = nn::linear(root / "wh", hidden, hidden, Default::
    default()); // W_h
let wy = nn::linear(root / "wy", hidden, vocab,  Default::
    default()); // W_y

let mut opt = nn::Adam::default().build(&vs, 1e-3)?; //
    optimizer
```

Shapes $W_x \in \mathbb{R}^{V \times H}$, $W_h \in \mathbb{R}^{H \times H}$, $W_y \in \mathbb{R}^{H \times V}$; $\mathbf{x}_t \in \mathbb{R}^{B \times V}$, $\mathbf{h}_t \in \mathbb{R}^{B \times H}$, $\mathbf{o}_t \in \mathbb{R}^{B \times V}$.

7.6.1.3   Step 3: Unrolled Forward Pass (Many to Many)

We iterate over time steps, update the hidden state, and collect logits for each step (Listing 7.4).

Listing 7.4 Forward unroll over T steps; collect logits per step

```rust
let (_x_idx, y_idx, x_oh) = make_batch(batch, t_steps, vocab,
    device);

// h_0 = 0 in (B, H)
let mut h = Tensor::zeros([batch, hidden], (Kind::Float, device
    ));

// collect (B, V) logits for each time step
let mut logits_per_t: Vec<Tensor> = Vec::with_capacity(t_steps
    as usize);

for t in 0..t_steps {
    // slice the t-th input: (B, 1, V) -> (B, V)
    let x_t = x_oh.narrow(1, t, 1).squeeze_dim(1);
```

```
13       // pre-activation: a_t = x_t @ W_x + h_{t-1} @ W_h
14       let a = x_t.apply(&wx) + h.apply(&wh);
15
16       // hidden update: h_t = tanh(a_t)
17       h = a.tanh();
18
19       // per-step logits: o_t = h_t @ W_y
20       let logits_t = h.apply(&wy); // (B, V)
21       logits_per_t.push(logits_t);
22   }
23
24   // stack back to (B, T, V)
25   let logits = Tensor::stack(&logits_per_t, 1);
```

Why This Mirrors the Math Each loop iteration is exactly one RNN time step; tanh is applied to the affine combination of the current input projection and the previous hidden state projection.

7.6.1.4 Step 4: Loss and BPTT (Automatic)

We reshape to apply cross-entropy over all steps and then let autograd backprop through the unrolled graph (Listing 7.5).

Listing 7.5 Cross-entropy over all steps and optimizer step

```
1  let loss = logits
2      .reshape([batch * t_steps, vocab])                 // (B*T, V)
3      .cross_entropy_for_logits(&y_idx.reshape([batch * t_steps])
           ); // (B*T)
4
5  opt.backward_step(&loss); // builds the graph across time and
       runs BPTT
```

What It Means CE is computed at every step and averaged over the batch; gradients flow through $\mathbf{o}_t \to \mathbf{h}_t \to \mathbf{h}_{t-1} \to \cdots$ thanks to autograd, i.e., full Backpropagation Through Time (BPTT).

7.6.1.5 Step 5: Monitoring Learning (Fixed eval Sample)

Every few epochs, we run a forward pass on a fixed $(B=1, T, V)$ sequence, decode argmax predictions, and compute accuracy in plain Rust (Listing 7.6).

Listing 7.6 Evaluation on a fixed sample and accuracy in Rust

```
1  let (_x_eval_idx, y_eval_idx, x_eval_oh) = make_batch(1,
       t_steps, vocab, device);
2
3  // ----- inside the epoch loop, every N epochs -----
4  let mut h_eval = Tensor::zeros([1, hidden], (Kind::Float,
       device));
```

```
5  let mut eval_logits_per_t: Vec<Tensor> = Vec::with_capacity(
       t_steps as usize);
6  for t in 0..t_steps {
7      let x_t = x_eval_oh.narrow(1, t, 1).squeeze_dim(1); // (1,
           V)
8      h_eval = (x_t.apply(&wx) + h_eval.apply(&wh)).tanh();
9      eval_logits_per_t.push(h_eval.apply(&wy));
10  }
11  let logits_eval = Tensor::stack(&eval_logits_per_t, 1);   // (1,
       T, V)
12  let preds = logits_eval.argmax(-1, false);                // (1,
       T)

13
14  // convert tensors to vectors and compute accuracy
15  let preds_vec: Vec<i64> = preds.to_device(Device::Cpu).view
       ([-1]).iter::<i64>()?.collect();
16  let y_vec:      Vec<i64> = y_eval_idx.to_device(Device::Cpu).view
       ([-1]).iter::<i64>()?.collect();
17  let correct = preds_vec.iter().zip(y_vec.iter()).filter(|(a,b)|
       a == b).count();
18  let acc = correct as f64 / preds_vec.len() as f64;

19
20  // pretty logging
21  let loss_val = loss.to_device(Device::Cpu).double_value(&[]);
22  println!("epoch {:3} | loss {:.4} | eval acc {:>5.1}%", epoch,
       loss_val, acc * 100.0);
```

Why Plain Rust for Accuracy In this tch version, we avoid tensor–tensor equality for metrics; converting to vectors is explicit and easy to follow in a book setting.

7.6.1.6 Step 6: End-to-End Training Loop (Skeleton)

For completeness, here is the canonical epoch structure (omitting the already-shown body for brevity) (Listing 7.7).

Listing 7.7 Epoch skeleton combining the previous steps

```
1  tch::manual_seed(42);
2  for epoch in 1..=epochs {
3      // (i) draw a fresh training batch
4      let (_x_idx, y_idx, x_oh) = make_batch(batch, t_steps,
           vocab, device);

5
6      // (ii) forward unroll over T -> logits (B, T, V)
7      // (iii) compute loss over (B*T, V)
8      // (iv) opt.backward_step(&loss);

9
10      // (v) every few epochs: run the fixed-sample evaluation
            (accuracy)
11  }
```

7.6.2   Reading the Output

Below is a real excerpt of the console output (loss and accuracy). It shows a consistent decrease in loss and an increase in accuracy to 100% on the fixed sample:

```
epoch  10 | loss 2.2279 | eval acc   0.0%
epoch  20 | loss 1.8359 | eval acc  25.0%
epoch  30 | loss 1.7515 | eval acc  37.5%
epoch  40 | loss 1.4042 | eval acc  62.5%

...

epoch  90 | loss 0.7931 | eval acc 100.0%
epoch 100 | loss 0.6308 | eval acc 100.0%

...

epoch 400 | loss 0.0250 | eval acc 100.0%
pred indices over time: [3, 4, 4, 2, 1, 4, 1, 2]
```

Interpretation

- *Loss* decreasing confirms correct forward/backward wiring and optimization.
- *Accuracy* reaching 100% (on this fixed sample) means the network learned the per-step mapping $x_t \mapsto (x_t + 1) \bmod V$, i.e., many-to-many classification.
- The final `pred indices` line prints one evaluated sequence's predicted classes over time.

7.6.3   How Each Line Mirrors the Equations

Per time step,

$$\underbrace{\mathbf{a}_t}_{a} = \mathbf{x}_t W_x + \mathbf{h}_{t-1} W_h \xrightarrow{\text{tanh}} \underbrace{\mathbf{h}_t}_{\texttt{h=a.tanh()}} \xrightarrow{\text{linear}} \underbrace{\mathbf{o}_t}_{\texttt{logits\_t=h.apply(\&wy)}} \xrightarrow{\text{CE}} \mathcal{L}_t.$$

Stacking $\mathbf{o}_t$ across t gives logits of shape (B, T, V), reshaped to (BT, V) for the cross-entropy. Autograd unrolls the graph across the time loop and applies BPTT when we call `backward_step`.

7.7   Long Short-Term Memory (LSTM)

While Recurrent Neural Networks (RNNs) are capable of modeling sequential dependencies, they often fail to capture *long-term dependencies* due to the **vanishing and exploding gradient problem**.

7.7.1   Why RNNs Struggle with Long-Term Dependencies

During training, RNNs apply *Backpropagation Through Time* (BPTT), which requires multiplying gradients by the same recurrent weight matrices at each time step. Over many time steps, these repeated multiplications can cause the gradient to either:

- Shrink toward zero (**vanishing gradient**), causing the network to "forget" long-range dependencies.
- Grow uncontrollably (**exploding gradient**), causing unstable training.

Intuitively, this happens because, in a standard RNN, the hidden state $\mathbf{h}(t)$ is overwritten at each step by a nonlinear transformation of $\mathbf{h}(t-1)$ and $\mathbf{x}(t)$. After many steps, information from the distant past becomes diluted or lost entirely.

7.7.2 The LSTM Solution

Long Short-Term Memory (LSTM) networks, introduced by Hochreiter and Schmidhuber [5], address this problem by introducing a separate **cell state** $\mathbf{c}(t)$ that acts as a memory channel. Instead of overwriting this state completely at each step, LSTMs use *gates* to control how much information to keep, update, and output.

This gating mechanism allows the LSTM to maintain information over long time spans, effectively mitigating the vanishing gradient problem.

7.7.3 Intuition Behind the Gates

An LSTM cell contains three main gates:

1. **Forget Gate** f_t: Decides what fraction of the old cell state $\mathbf{c}(t-1)$ to keep.
2. **Input Gate** i_t: Decides how much new candidate information $\tilde{\mathbf{c}}_t$ to add to the cell state.
3. **Output Gate** o_t: Decides how much of the cell state to expose to the hidden state $\mathbf{h}(t)$ (and thus to the next layer or output).

In plain English:

- The *forget gate* controls what to "erase" from memory.
- The *input gate* controls what to "write" into memory.
- The *output gate* controls what to "read" from memory.

7.7.4 Mathematical Formulation

Given the input vector $\mathbf{x}_t$, previous hidden state $\mathbf{h}_{t-1}$, and previous cell state $\mathbf{c}_{t-1}$, an LSTM cell computes:

$$f_t = \sigma(W_f \mathbf{x}_t + U_f \mathbf{h}_{t-1} + b_f) \quad \text{(forget gate)}$$

$$i_t = \sigma(W_i \mathbf{x}_t + U_i \mathbf{h}_{t-1} + b_i) \quad \text{(input gate)}$$

$$\tilde{\mathbf{c}}_t = \tanh(W_c \mathbf{x}_t + U_c \mathbf{h}_{t-1} + b_c) \quad \text{(candidate cell state)}$$

$$\mathbf{c}_t = f_t \odot \mathbf{c}_{t-1} + i_t \odot \tilde{\mathbf{c}}_t \quad \text{(new cell state)}$$

$$o_t = \sigma(W_o \mathbf{x}_t + U_o \mathbf{h}_{t-1} + b_o) \quad \text{(output gate)}$$

$$\mathbf{h}_t = o_t \odot \tanh(\mathbf{c}_t) \quad \text{(new hidden state)}$$

where:

- $\sigma(\cdot)$ is the sigmoid activation function.
- $\tanh(\cdot)$ is the hyperbolic tangent activation.
- $\odot$ denotes elementwise multiplication.
- $W., U., b.$ are learnable parameters.

7.7.5   Training LSTMs

Training an LSTM follows the same principle as training an RNN:

1. Define a loss function over the output sequence (e.g., cross-entropy for classification tasks).
2. Perform a forward pass over all time steps to compute $\mathbf{h}_t$ and $\mathbf{c}_t$.
3. Apply **Backpropagation Through Time (BPTT)**, which now includes gradients through both the hidden state $\mathbf{h}_t$ and the cell state $\mathbf{c}_t$.
4. Update parameters using gradient descent or an adaptive optimizer (e.g., Adam).

Thanks to the linear additive update of the cell state, $\mathbf{c}_t = f_t \odot \mathbf{c}_{t-1} + \ldots$, the gradient can flow backward over many time steps with much less decay, enabling the network to learn long-term dependencies.

7.7.6   Architecture

Figure 7.9 illustrates the internal structure of an LSTM cell, including the forget, input, and output gates, as well as the flow of the cell state $\mathbf{c}_t$ and hidden state $\mathbf{h}_t$.

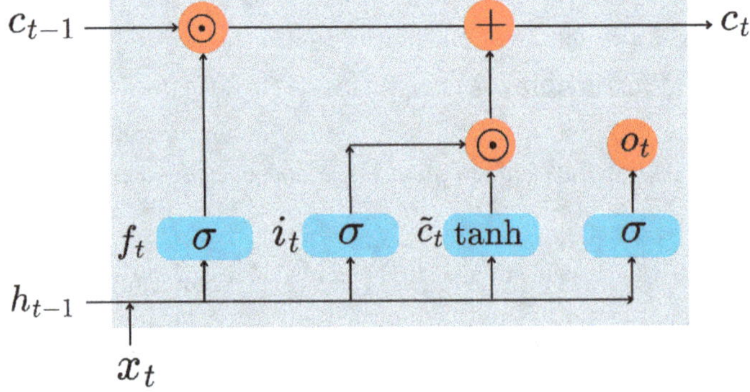

Figure 7.9 LSTM

7.8   Implementing LSTM in Rust over the One-Shift Example

Goal We reuse the exact same toy task as in the RNN section: given a token sequence $x_{1:T}$ over a vocabulary of size V (one-hot inputs), predict at each step the *shift-by-1* label

$$y_t = (x_t + 1) \bmod V, \qquad t = 1, \ldots, T.$$

The training loop, loss (cross-entropy over all steps), and evaluation logic remain *unchanged*. We only replace the recurrent cell: from a manual tanh RNN to an LSTM.

7.8.1   What Stays the Same

- **Data generation** (random tokens $\rightarrow$ one-hot inputs), **batch shapes** (B, T, V), and **labels** (B, T).
- **Loss:** Reshape logits to (BT, V) and labels to (BT), apply cross-entropy.
- **Optimizer:** Adam (same LR).
- **Evaluation:** argmax per time step, accuracy computed by comparing predicted vs. target indices.
- **Output head:** A linear map $W_y : \mathbb{R}^H \to \mathbb{R}^V$ applied at each time step.

7.8.2   What Changes (and Why)

Why LSTM?
A vanilla RNN updates $\mathbf{h}_t = \tanh(\mathbf{x}_t W_x + \mathbf{h}_{t-1} W_h + \mathbf{b}_h)$. An LSTM augments this with a *cell state* $\mathbf{c}_t$ and gating (input/forget/output) to regulate information flow:

$$\mathbf{i}_t = \sigma(\mathbf{x}_t W_{xi} + \mathbf{h}_{t-1} W_{hi} + \mathbf{b}_i), \quad \mathbf{f}_t = \sigma(\cdot), \quad \mathbf{o}_t = \sigma(\cdot),$$

$$\mathbf{g}_t = \tanh(\cdot), \qquad \mathbf{c}_t = \mathbf{f}_t \odot \mathbf{c}_{t-1} + \mathbf{i}_t \odot \mathbf{g}_t, \qquad \mathbf{h}_t = \mathbf{o}_t \odot \tanh(\mathbf{c}_t).$$

This gating helps with longer dependencies and stabilizes training.

Code Swap
Replace the *manual* RNN cell (two linears + `tanh` in a time loop) with `nn::lstm` and keep the rest intact.

7.8.3   The Minimal Changes, Shown Side by Side

(A) Cell Definition
Before (RNN)

```
let wx = nn::linear(root / "wx", vocab,  hidden, Default::
    default());
let wh = nn::linear(root / "wh", hidden, hidden, Default::
    default());
let wy = nn::linear(root / "wy", hidden, vocab,  Default::
    default());
```

After (LSTM)

```
1  let lstm = nn::lstm(
2      root / "lstm",
3      vocab,  // input size (I = V)
4      hidden, // hidden size (H)
5      nn::RNNConfig {
6          num_layers: 1,
7          bidirectional: false,
8          batch_first: true, // we feed (B,T,I)
9          ..Default::default()
10     },
11 );
12 let wy = nn::linear(root / "wy", hidden, vocab, Default::
       default());
```

Why nn::lstm encapsulates gate math and the cell state. We set batch_first=true so inputs stay in the convenient shape (B, T, V) throughout.

(B) Forward Pass (Unroll)
Before (RNN)

```
1  // h_0 = zeros(B,H); loop t=0..T-1
2  let x_t = x_oh.narrow(1, t, 1).squeeze_dim(1);  // (B,V)
3  let a = x_t.apply(&wx) + h.apply(&wh);
4  h = a.tanh();                          // (B,H)
5  let logits_t = h.apply(&wy);  // (B,V)
6  ...
7  let logits = Tensor::stack(&logits_per_t, 1);  // (B,T,V)
```

After (LSTM)

```
1  // Input x_oh: (B,T,V) because batch_first=true
2  let (h_seq, _state) = lstm.seq(&x_oh);  // (B,T,H)
3  let logits = h_seq.apply(&wy);          // (B,T,V)
```

Why With LSTM, we no longer hand-roll the time loop; lstm.seq unrolls internally (and autograd performs BPTT through it).

(C) Loss and Optimizer (Unchanged)

```
1  // logits: (B,T,V), y_idx: (B,T)
2  let loss = logits
3      .reshape([batch * t_steps, vocab])                // (BT, V)
4      .cross_entropy_for_logits(&y_idx.reshape([batch * t_steps]));
           // (BT)
5  opt.backward_step(&loss); // full BPTT handled by autograd
```

(D) Evaluation (Unchanged)

```
1   // fixed eval sample x_eval_oh: (1,T,V)
2   let (h_eval, _st) = lstm.seq(&x_eval_oh);    // (1,T,H)
3   let logits_eval = h_eval.apply(&wy);         // (1,T,V)
4   let preds = logits_eval.argmax(-1, false);   // (1,T)
5   // convert to Vec<i64> and compare with targets for accuracy
```

7.8.4   Reading the Results

Because the task is easy, both RNN and LSTM often reach 100% accuracy eventually. However, the LSTM usually reaches high accuracy *faster and more stably*, thanks to its gating and cell state. A typical printout you might see:

```
epoch   10 | loss 1.7266 | eval acc   37.5%
...
epoch  100 | loss 1.3891 | eval acc 100.0%
...
pred indices over time: [0, 1, 2, 3, 3, 3, 2, 1]
```

The "pred indices" line lists the predicted class at each time step for the fixed evaluation sequence; matching the ground truth exactly explains the 100% accuracy.

7.8.5   Recap

To implement an **LSTM** over the same one-shift example:

1. Swap the manual RNN cell for `nn::lstm` with `batch_first=true`.
2. Feed inputs as (B, T, V) into `lstm.seq`, and then apply the same linear head W_y at each step.
3. Keep the loss, optimizer, and evaluation code unchanged.

This isolates the architectural change to the recurrent cell while preserving the rest of the training pipeline, making the comparison with the vanilla RNN clean and fair.

Summary

In this chapter, we explored three fundamental deep learning architectures in Rust using the `tch` crate: Convolutional Neural Networks (CNNs), Recurrent Neural Networks (RNNs), and Long Short-Term Memory networks (LSTMs).

We began with CNNs, which are widely used for image processing tasks. We covered convolutional layers, activation functions, pooling layers, and fully connected layers, showing how spatial feature extraction works efficiently in Rust.

Next, we implemented a vanilla RNN for a simple one-shift sequence prediction problem. This example demonstrated how hidden states evolve over time and how RNNs can capture sequential patterns, albeit with limitations in handling long-term dependencies.

Finally, we replaced the RNN with an LSTM to overcome the vanishing gradient problem. By introducing gating mechanisms (input, forget, and output gates) and a separate cell state, the LSTM learned more robustly and retained information over longer sequences. The same dataset and training loop were used for both RNN and LSTM, allowing a direct performance comparison.

Problems

7.1 Simple CNN on MNIST: Implement a CNN in Rust to classify digits from the MNIST dataset:[1]

1. Use one convolutional layer followed by a pooling layer and a fully connected layer.
2. Train for at least three epochs and print the accuracy after training.

7.2 RNN vs. LSTM on Short Sequence: Using a simple sequence prediction task (e.g., predicting the next number in a short numeric pattern):

1. Train both a vanilla RNN and an LSTM with the same data.
2. Compare their accuracy after training for 50 epochs.

7.3 Conceptual: Choosing the Right Architecture: For each of the following application scenarios, explain whether CNN, RNN, or LSTM is most appropriate and why:

- Handwritten digit recognition.
- Predicting the next word in a sentence.
- Detecting anomalies in sensor data streams.

---

[1] https://www.kaggle.com/datasets/hojjatk/mnist-dataset

Chapter 8
Generative Models and Transformers in Rust

8.1 Introduction

This chapter introduces two foundational architectures in modern deep learning: Generative Adversarial Networks (GANs) and Transformers. We provide minimal, runnable Rust implementations of each, highlighting their core components and training processes. The GAN section focuses on the interplay between generator and discriminator in producing realistic outputs, while the Transformer section demonstrates self-attention, positional encoding, and multi-head attention through a synthetic sequence classification task. Although the Transformer experiment is small-scale and achieves limited accuracy, it effectively illustrates the mechanisms that enable attention-based models to capture global dependencies.

Chapter Goal

The goal of this chapter is to give readers a practical, implementation-focused understanding of GANs and Transformers, showing how their key building blocks operate in code. By the end, readers should be able to recognize the essential architecture of each model, understand their training workflows, and appreciate why large-scale compute and data are required for state-of-the-art results.

8.2 Generative Adversarial Network (GAN)

In previous chapters, we have dealt with supervised learning, which relies on a training set consisting of pairs of (input, output) data to predict the output for unseen input data. However, the **Generative Adversarial Network (GAN)**, introduced by Goodfellow et al. [3], is an unsupervised machine learning model that can generate new data that closely resembles the training dataset, without any labels or explicit guidance on what to generate.

These models have found applications in various domains, including the controversial use in deepfake technology to create fake images, voices, text, and more. Unfortunately, many malicious actors have misused this technology for fraudulent purposes. For example, a report in *The Wall Street Journal* described how the CEO of a UK-based energy firm, believing he was speaking with his boss, the chief executive of the company's German parent, followed instructions to immediately transfer €220,000 (approximately \$243,000) to a Hungarian supplier's bank account.[1]

---

[1] https://www.wsj.com/articles/fraudsters-use-ai-to-mimic-ceos-voice-in-unusual-cybercrime-case-11567157402

M. Maleki, *Deep Learning with Rust*, https://doi.org/10.1007/979-8-8688-2208-7_8

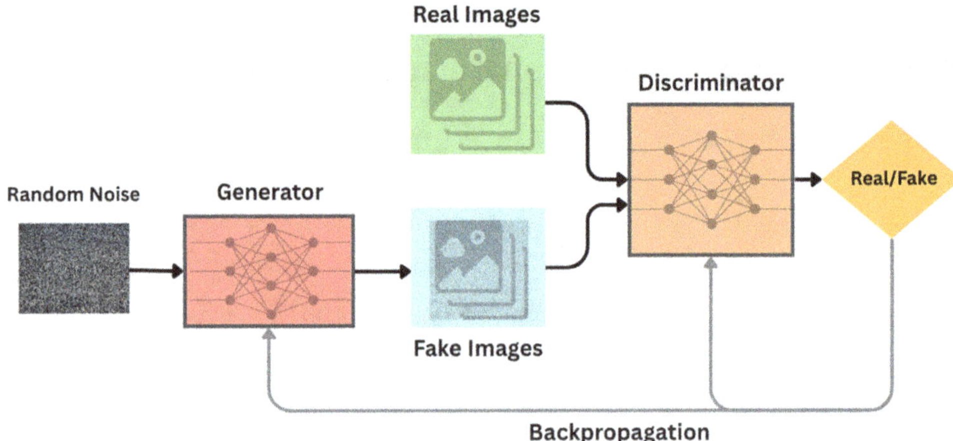

Figure 8.1 The architecture of a Generative Adversarial Network (GAN), consisting of a generator that produces fake data and a discriminator that classifies data as real or fake. The generator and discriminator are trained in a min-max game, where the generator aims to fool the discriminator and the discriminator seeks to correctly distinguish between real and fake data

But how does this model work, and how can it generate fake data, such as images, that are indistinguishable from real ones? The answer lies in two key components of the GAN: the **generator** and the **discriminator**.

- The **generator** creates random data from a random probability distribution, known as the *latent space*.
- The **discriminator**, a supervised machine learning model, is trained on real data to determine whether the input data is real or fake.

The process involves a feedback loop: the generator produces fake data, and the discriminator attempts to detect whether it is real or fake. If the discriminator successfully identifies the fake data, the feedback is used to improve the generator's output, thereby reducing the chance of rejection by the discriminator. This iterative process continues until the generator "defeats" the discriminator by producing data that cannot be distinguished from real data.

The architecture of the GAN is illustrated in Figure 8.1.

Mathematically, let z be the latent variable (input noise) and x be the generated signal by the generator. The GAN optimization problem is framed as follows:

$$\min_{G} \max_{D} V(D, G) = \mathbb{E}_{x \sim p_{data}(x)}[\log D(x)] + \mathbb{E}_{z \sim p_z(z)}[\log(1 - D(G(z)))]$$

This equation represents a **min-max** game between two components of the GAN: the **generator (G)** and the **discriminator (D)**.

8.2.1 Min-Max Game

$$\min_{G} \max_{D} V(D, G)$$

- $\min_G$: The generator G seeks to minimize the value of the function $V(D, G)$. Its goal is to generate data that closely resembles real data, making it harder for the discriminator to distinguish between real and fake.
- $\max_D$: The discriminator D aims to maximize the value of the function $V(D, G)$. Its goal is to correctly classify real data as real and fake data as fake.

Thus, this is a **min-max** game, a typical setup for GANs. The generator tries to fool the discriminator, and the discriminator tries to correctly classify real and fake data. The process continues until both the generator and discriminator reach an equilibrium.

8.2.2   Expectation for Real Data x

$$\mathbb{E}_{x \sim p_{data}(x)}[\log D(x)]$$

- $\mathbb{E}$: This represents the expectation (average) over the real data distribution.
- $x \sim p_{data}(x)$: The variable x is sampled from the real data distribution $p_{data}(x)$.
- $\log D(x)$: $D(x)$ is the discriminator's output, which represents the probability that the input data x is real. The log is taken to facilitate gradient-based optimization.
- The goal for the discriminator is to output $D(x) \approx 1$ for real data, and the log of 1 is 0, which makes the term large (maximal).

This term represents how well the discriminator can correctly classify real data. The discriminator aims to maximize this term, making the classification of real data more accurate.

8.2.3   Expectation for Fake Data G(z)

$$\mathbb{E}_{z \sim p_z(z)}[\log(1 - D(G(z)))]$$

- $z \sim p_z(z)$: The variable z is sampled from the latent space distribution $p_z(z)$, which is random noise given as input to the generator.
- $G(z)$: The generator G produces fake data from the latent variable z.
- $\log(1 - D(G(z)))$: This term represents the discriminator's output for the fake data generated by $G(z)$. The generator aims to minimize $D(G(z))$, pushing the discriminator to classify fake data as fake (i.e., $D(G(z)) \approx 0$).

This term represents how well the generator produces fake data that the discriminator classifies as fake. The generator seeks to minimize this term, trying to fool the discriminator into thinking that the generated data is real.

8.2.4   Objective Function Interpretation

- **Generator's Goal**: The generator G seeks to minimize the objective function, i.e., make the discriminator more likely to classify the fake data as real. By doing so, the generator learns to generate more realistic data.
- **Discriminator's Goal**: The discriminator D seeks to maximize the objective function, i.e., it wants to correctly identify real data as real and fake data as fake.

8.2.5   The Min-Max Problem

This equation represents a **min-max** optimization problem because the generator and discriminator are in competition. The generator tries to fool the discriminator by producing realistic fake data, while the discriminator tries to accurately classify real and fake data. The equilibrium is achieved when the generator produces data indistinguishable from real data, and the discriminator cannot distinguish between the two.

8.2.6   Equilibrium

The ultimate goal of the GAN is for both the generator and the discriminator to reach an equilibrium. At this equilibrium, the generator is able to produce fake data that is indistinguishable from real data, and the discriminator has no advantage in distinguishing real from fake data. Both the generator and the discriminator adjust their weights during training, and the game continues until the generator reaches an optimal state where the discriminator cannot improve further.

Thus, the problem faced by both the generator and discriminator is to solve this optimization problem. The generator aims to "fool" the discriminator by producing increasingly realistic fake data, while the discriminator aims to accurately differentiate real from fake. The game continues until the generator reaches an equilibrium where its generated data is indistinguishable from real data.

8.3   A Minimal GAN in Rust with tch: Explanation and Walk-Through

This section documents a compact, working implementation of a Generative Adversarial Network (GAN) in Rust using the tch crate (PyTorch bindings). The goal is to learn a simple 2D target distribution: a mixture of two Gaussians centered near $(-2, 0)$ and $(2, 0)$. The *generator G* maps Gaussian noise z to 2D points, and the *discriminator D* receives 2D points and outputs a logit indicating "real" vs. "fake." We alternate updates to D and G using the standard GAN minimax losses (implemented with numerically stable log-sigmoid forms).

8.3.1   High-Level Flow

1. Sample a batch of *real* points from the target 2D mixture.
2. Sample a batch of *noise* $z \sim \mathcal{N}(0, I)$, and push through G to get *fake* points.
3. Update D to increase its score on real and decrease its score on fake.
4. Update G to increase D's score on generated points (fool D).
5. Repeat, log losses, and finally sample a few generated points.

8.3.2   *Full Code (for Reference)*

```rust
use tch::{nn, nn::Module, nn::ModuleT, nn::OptimizerConfig,
    Device, Kind, Tensor};

/// Sample a batch of real data: 2D mixture of two Gaussians.
fn sample_real(batch: i64, device: Device) -> Tensor {
    let half = batch / 2;
    let std = 0.5_f64; // use f64 for scalar ops

    // Means as tensors (Float32 is fine; broadcasting will
        work)
    let mean1 = Tensor::f_from_slice(&[-2.0f32, 0.0]).unwrap()
        .to_device(device)
        .view([1, 2]);
    let mean2 = Tensor::f_from_slice(&[ 2.0f32, 0.0]).unwrap()
        .to_device(device)
        .view([1, 2]);

    let x1 = Tensor::randn([half, 2], (Kind::Float, device)) *
        std + &mean1;          // (half,2)
    let x2 = Tensor::randn([batch - half, 2], (Kind::Float,
        device)) * std + &mean2; // (batch-half,2)
    Tensor::cat(&[x1, x2], 0) // (batch,2)
}

/// Generator: z_dim -> 64 -> 2
fn build_generator(vs: &nn::Path, z_dim: i64) -> nn::Sequential
    {
    nn::seq()
        .add(nn::linear(vs / "g1", z_dim, 64, Default::default
            ()))
        .add_fn(|xs| xs.relu())
        .add(nn::linear(vs / "g2", 64, 2, Default::default()))
}

/// Discriminator: 2 -> 64 -> 1 (logit)
fn build_discriminator(vs: &nn::Path) -> nn::Sequential {
    nn::seq()
        .add(nn::linear(vs / "d1", 2, 64, Default::default()))
        .add_fn(|xs| xs.leaky_relu()) // no alpha argument in
            tch 0.18
        .add(nn::linear(vs / "d2", 64, 1, Default::default()))
}

fn main() {
    // Reproducibility + device
    tch::manual_seed(42);
    let device = Device::cuda_if_available();
```

```rust
41    println!("Running on: {:?}", device);
42
43    // Separate var stores (so G and D have separate optimizers
      )
44    let vs_g = nn::VarStore::new(device);
45    let vs_d = nn::VarStore::new(device);
46
47    // Hyperparams
48    let z_dim: i64 = 8;
49    let batch: i64 = 128;
50    let iters: i64 = 2000;
51    let print_every: i64 = 100;
52
53    // Models
54    let g = build_generator(&vs_g.root(), z_dim);
55    let d = build_discriminator(&vs_d.root());
56
57    // Optimizers
58    let mut opt_g = nn::Adam::default().build(&vs_g, 2e-4).
      unwrap();
59    let mut opt_d = nn::Adam::default().build(&vs_d, 2e-4).
      unwrap();
60
61    for step in 1..=iters {
62        // -----------------------------
63        // Train Discriminator
64        // -----------------------------
65        let x_real = sample_real(batch, device); // (B,2)
66        let z = Tensor::randn([batch, z_dim], (Kind::Float,
          device));
67        let x_fake = g.forward_t(&z, true);        // (B,2)
68
69        let d_real_logits = d.forward_t(&x_real, true);
                  // (B,1)
70        let d_fake_logits = d.forward_t(&x_fake.detach(), true)
          ; // (B,1)
71
72        // BCE-with-logits (stable): -log (a) - log(1- (b)) = -
          log (a) - log (-b)
73        let loss_d_real = -d_real_logits.log_sigmoid().mean(
          Kind::Float);
74        let loss_d_fake = -(-&d_fake_logits).log_sigmoid().mean
          (Kind::Float);
75        let loss_d = &loss_d_real + &loss_d_fake;
76
77        opt_d.backward_step(&loss_d);
78
79        // -----------------------------
80        // Train Generator
81        // -----------------------------
```

```rust
82          let z2 = Tensor::randn([batch, z_dim], (Kind::Float,
                device));
83          let x_fake2 = g.forward_t(&z2, true);
84          let d_fake2_logits = d.forward_t(&x_fake2, true);

86          // G wants D to predict "real" for fakes: minimize -log
               (D(G(z)))
87          let loss_g = -d_fake2_logits.log_sigmoid().mean(Kind::
               Float);

89          opt_g.backward_step(&loss_g);

91          if step % print_every == 0 {
92              let ld = loss_d.to_device(Device::Cpu).double_value
                   (&[]);
93              let lg = loss_g.to_device(Device::Cpu).double_value
                   (&[]);
94              println!("step {:4} | d_loss {:.4} | g_loss {:.4}",
                   step, ld, lg);
95          }
96      }

98      // Sample a few points from the trained generator
99      let z = Tensor::randn([10, z_dim], (Kind::Float, device));
100     let samples = g.forward_t(&z, false).to_device(Device::Cpu)
           ; // (10,2)
101     let flat: Vec<f32> = samples.view([-1]).try_into().unwrap()
           ;
102     println!("generated samples (x,y):");
103     for i in 0..10 {
104         let x = flat[2 * i];
105         let y = flat[2 * i + 1];
106         println!("  {:>2}: [{:.3}, {:.3}]", i, x, y);
107     }
108 }
```

8.3.3   *Explaining Each Part*

Imports and Traits

```rust
1  use tch::{nn, nn::Module, nn::ModuleT, nn::OptimizerConfig,
       Device, Kind, Tensor};
```

We bring into scope:

- nn::Module / nn::ModuleT for .forward() / .forward_t() on nn::Sequential.
- OptimizerConfig to build Adam optimizers.
- Device, Kind, Tensor for tensor creation and device control.

Sampling Real Data (Target Distribution)

```
1  fn sample_real(batch: i64, device: Device) -> Tensor { ... }
```

This function draws a mini-batch of 2D points from a mixture of two Gaussians: half near $(-2, 0)$ and half near $(2, 0)$. We use:

$$X \sim \tfrac{1}{2}\mathcal{N}((-2, 0), \sigma^2 I) + \tfrac{1}{2}\mathcal{N}((2, 0), \sigma^2 I),$$

with $\sigma = 0.5$. The returned tensor has shape $(B, 2)$ on the requested device.

Model Definitions

```
1  fn build_generator(vs: &nn::Path, z_dim: i64) -> nn::Sequential
       { ... }
2  fn build_discriminator(vs: &nn::Path) -> nn::Sequential { ... }
```

- **Generator** G: An MLP mapping $z \in \mathbb{R}^{z\_dim} \to \mathbb{R}^2$. Architecture: `Linear(z_dim, 64)` + ReLU + `Linear(64, 2)`.
- **Discriminator** D: An MLP mapping $x \in \mathbb{R}^2 \to$ logit in $\mathbb{R}$. Architecture: `Linear(2, 64)` + LeakyReLU + `Linear(64, 1)`.

Both are built under their own `VarStore` so we can optimize them independently.

Main Setup

```
1  tch::manual_seed(42);
2  let device = Device::cuda_if_available();
3  let vs_g = nn::VarStore::new(device);
4  let vs_d = nn::VarStore::new(device);
5  let z_dim = 8; let batch = 128; let iters = 2000;
6  let g = build_generator(&vs_g.root(), z_dim);
7  let d = build_discriminator(&vs_d.root());
8  let mut opt_g = nn::Adam::default().build(&vs_g, 2e-4).unwrap()
       ;
9  let mut opt_d = nn::Adam::default().build(&vs_d, 2e-4).unwrap()
       ;
```

We set seeds for reproducibility, pick device (CPU or CUDA), build models and optimizers, and define hyperparameters.

Training the Discriminator

```
1  let x_real = sample_real(batch, device);              // (B,2)
2  let z = Tensor::randn([batch, z_dim], (Kind::Float, device));
3  let x_fake = g.forward_t(&z, true);                   // (B,2)
4  let d_real_logits = d.forward_t(&x_real, true);       // (B,1)
5  let d_fake_logits = d.forward_t(&x_fake.detach(), true);
6  let loss_d_real = -d_real_logits.log_sigmoid().mean(Kind::Float
       );
7  let loss_d_fake = -(-&d_fake_logits).log_sigmoid().mean(Kind::
       Float);
```

```
8   let loss_d = &loss_d_real + &loss_d_fake;
9   opt_d.backward_step(&loss_d);
```

- We generate real and fake batches and pass both through D to obtain logits.
- The discriminator objective (BCE with logits) in a numerically stable form:

$$\mathcal{L}_D = -\log \sigma(D(x_{\text{real}})) - \log \sigma(-D(G(z))).$$

- We *detach* x_{fake} so the generator is not updated during D's step.

Training the Generator

```
1   let z2 = Tensor::randn([batch, z_dim], (Kind::Float, device));
2   let x_fake2 = g.forward_t(&z2, true);
3   let d_fake2_logits = d.forward_t(&x_fake2, true);
4   let loss_g = -d_fake2_logits.log_sigmoid().mean(Kind::Float);
5   opt_g.backward_step(&loss_g);
```

The generator wants to maximize D's belief that fake samples are real:

$$\mathcal{L}_G = -\log \sigma(D(G(z))).$$

No detach here—gradients flow through D into G.

Logging and Scalars in `tch`

```
1   let ld = loss_d.to_device(Device::Cpu).double_value(&[]);
2   let lg = loss_g.to_device(Device::Cpu).double_value(&[]);
3   println!("step {:4} | d_loss {:.4} | g_loss {:.4}", step, ld,
        lg);
```

In `tch` 0.18, extract scalar tensor values with `.double_value(&[])` (or `.float_value(&[])`),
not `f64::from(tensor)`.

Sampling from the Trained Generator

```
1   let z = Tensor::randn([10, z_dim], (Kind::Float, device));
2   let samples = g.forward_t(&z, false).to_device(Device::Cpu); //
        (10,2)
3   let flat: Vec<f32> = samples.view([-1]).try_into().unwrap();
4   for i in 0..10 {
5       println!("  {:>2}: [{:.3}, {:.3}]", i, flat[2*i], flat[2*i
            + 1]);
6   }
```

We draw new noise, map through G, and print coordinates. You should see points near both clusters
as training progresses.

8.3.4   Notes and Tips

- **Stability:** GANs can be unstable. If losses diverge, try reducing LR (e.g., $2 \cdot 10^{-4} \to 1 \cdot 10^{-4}$) or increasing batch size.
- **Capacity:** Increase hidden size (e.g., $64 \to 128$) for a tighter fit to the two Gaussians.
- **Visualization:** For a quick scatter plot, save real/fake samples to CSV and plot in Python/Matplotlib or Excel.
- **tch Specifics:**

  1. Bring `nn::Module` and `nn::ModuleT` into scope to use `.forward()` and `.forward_t()`.
  2. Use `.log_sigmoid()` (underscore) in 0.18 for stable BCE with logits.
  3. Prefer `f64` scalars with tensors where needed (e.g., `0.5_f64`).

8.3.5   What Success Looks Like

During training you should see discriminator and generator losses hovering in a competitive range (e.g., $D \in [1.0, 1.4]$, $G \in [0.7, 1.2]$ for this toy task). Generated samples printed at the end should include several points near both cluster centers, indicating that G has learned a simple multimodal distribution.

8.3.6   Result Interpretation

The training output for the CPU run is as follows:

```
Running on: Cpu
step   100 | d_loss 1.2582 | g_loss 1.2021
step   200 | d_loss 1.1054 | g_loss 1.0465
step   300 | d_loss 1.0738 | g_loss 0.9846
step   400 | d_loss 1.0401 | g_loss 0.9944
step   500 | d_loss 1.0241 | g_loss 1.0124
step   600 | d_loss 1.0091 | g_loss 1.0272
step   700 | d_loss 1.0070 | g_loss 1.0396
step   800 | d_loss 1.1176 | g_loss 0.9270
step   900 | d_loss 1.2840 | g_loss 0.7944
step  1000 | d_loss 1.3622 | g_loss 0.7892
step  1100 | d_loss 1.3708 | g_loss 0.8012
step  1200 | d_loss 1.3475 | g_loss 0.8312
step  1300 | d_loss 1.3308 | g_loss 0.8084
step  1400 | d_loss 1.3077 | g_loss 0.7507
step  1500 | d_loss 1.3693 | g_loss 0.7595
step  1600 | d_loss 1.3571 | g_loss 0.7438
step  1700 | d_loss 1.3457 | g_loss 0.7219
step  1800 | d_loss 1.3462 | g_loss 0.7357
step  1900 | d_loss 1.2576 | g_loss 0.7674
step  2000 | d_loss 1.2891 | g_loss 0.7998
```

At the start of training (steps 100–300), both the discriminator loss ($\mathcal{L}_D$) and generator loss ($\mathcal{L}_G$) are relatively high (≈ 1.2 and ≈ 1.0, respectively), reflecting the fact that both models are still learning. By steps 500–700, $\mathcal{L}_D$ hovers around 1.0 and $\mathcal{L}_G$ also stays near 1.0, indicating a temporary balance where the discriminator correctly identifies some fakes but not all, and the generator is moderately successful in fooling it.

From step 800 onward, $\mathcal{L}_D$ increases slightly above 1.2 while $\mathcal{L}_G$ decreases toward 0.75–0.8. This suggests the generator is producing more realistic samples, causing the discriminator to work harder and occasionally misclassify fakes as real. The fluctuations in both losses are expected in GAN training and reflect the adversarial nature of the optimization.

The final generated samples after 2000 steps are:

```
generated samples (x,y):
    0: [-0.416,  0.173]
    1: [-0.323,  0.237]
    2: [ 1.351, -0.047]
    3: [-0.558,  0.086]
    4: [ 0.371,  0.288]
    5: [-0.972,  0.005]
    6: [ 0.307,  0.357]
    7: [-1.749,  0.895]
    8: [-2.599, -0.228]
    9: [ 2.095,  0.641]
```

These points are distributed across both modes of the target distribution:

- Samples like $(-2.599, -0.228)$ and $(-1.749, 0.895)$ are close to the left Gaussian centered near $(-2, 0)$.
- Samples like $(2.095, 0.641)$ and $(1.351, -0.047)$ are near the right Gaussian centered at $(2, 0)$.
- Several points lie in between modes, which can happen in early stage GANs with small networks, but the clustering indicates the generator has learned the bimodal structure.

Overall, the training log and generated samples confirm that the minimal GAN successfully captured the basic geometry of the two-cluster target distribution within 2000 iterations on CPU. The visual evidence of this learning process is clearly illustrated in Figure 8.2, where the generated samples (red crosses) align closely with the two Gaussian clusters (blue points) representing the true data distribution.

8.4   Transformers

Imagine translating a sentence from English to French, such as converting "The cat sat on the mat" into "Le chat s'est assis sur le tapis." A translation model must understand which words in the input correspond to which words in the output—for example, that "cat" maps to "chat," and that "on the mat" together becomes "sur le tapis." Traditional recurrent neural networks (RNNs) process such sentences one word at a time, making it difficult to capture long-distance relationships (e.g., between "cat" and "mat"). Transformers, by contrast, model all relationships between words simultaneously using the **attention mechanism**, which learns how strongly each word should attend to every other word in the sequence.

Transformers are a class of neural network architectures that rely entirely on attention to model dependencies between input and output sequences. Unlike recurrent neural networks (RNNs) or convolutional neural networks (CNNs), Transformers dispense with both recurrence and convolution.

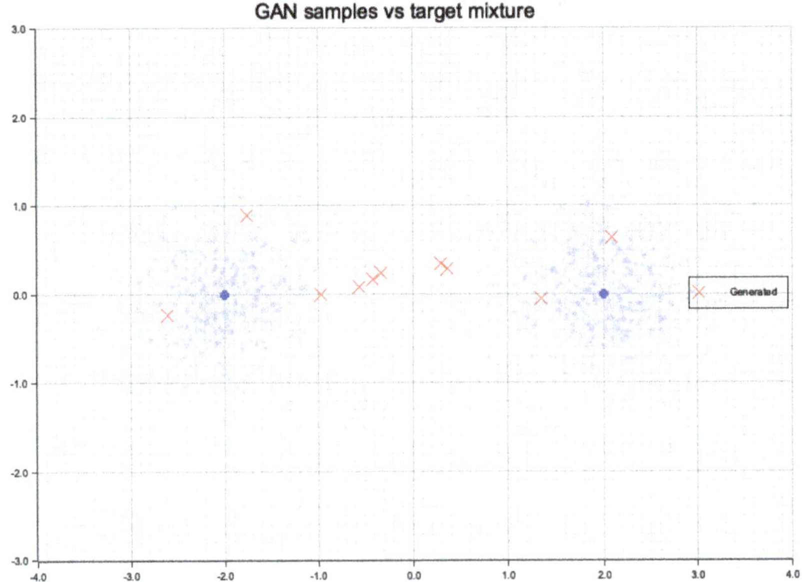

Figure 8.2 Generated samples (red crosses) over the true bimodal Gaussian mixture (blue points)

This design enables highly parallelizable training and allows the model to capture long-range dependencies far more effectively. Over the next sections, we will use this translation example to illustrate how attention works, how Transformers process input sequences, and how they achieve state-of-the-art performance across natural language processing and beyond.

8.4.1 Architecture Overview

The original Transformer, proposed by Vaswani et al. [10], consists of an **encoder-decoder** structure:

- **Encoder:** A stack of identical layers, each containing a multi-head self-attention mechanism and a position-wise feed-forward network.
- **Decoder:** Also a stack of identical layers, but each layer has an additional encoder-decoder attention mechanism to incorporate encoder outputs.

8.4.2 Self-Attention Mechanism

Self-attention is the **core operation** that enables a Transformer to model relationships between *any* pair of positions in a sequence, regardless of their distance. Given an input sequence of token embeddings

$$\mathbf{X} \in \mathbb{R}^{n \times d_{\text{model}}},$$

where n is the sequence length and d_{model} is the embedding dimension, we compute three projected versions of $\mathbf{X}$:

$$Q = \mathbf{X}W_Q, \tag{8.1}$$

$$K = \mathbf{X}W_K, \tag{8.2}$$

$$V = \mathbf{X}W_V, \tag{8.3}$$

where

$$W_Q, W_K, W_V \in \mathbb{R}^{d_{\text{model}} \times d_k}$$

are learnable parameter matrices that map the same input $\mathbf{X}$ into three different spaces:

- Q (Queries): "What am I looking for in other tokens?"
- K (Keys): "What do I have that others might find relevant?"
- V (Values): "What information will I pass along if I am attended to?"

Similarity Computation

For each token, attention measures how *similar* its query is to the keys of other tokens. The similarity score between token i and token j is given by the dot product $Q_i K_j^\top$. Scaling by $\sqrt{d_k}$ stabilizes gradients when d_k is large:

$$\text{scores} = \frac{QK^\top}{\sqrt{d_k}} \quad \in \mathbb{R}^{n \times n}.$$

Softmax Weighting

We convert the raw attention scores into a probability distribution over all tokens using the softmax function:

$$\text{weights}_{ij} = \frac{\exp(\text{scores}_{ij})}{\sum_{m=1}^{n} \exp(\text{scores}_{im})}.$$

Here, weights_{ij} indicates how much information token i should take from token j. The softmax ensures that, for each i, all weights sum to 1, creating a normalized distribution of attention across the sequence. This normalization is crucial because it allows the model to *blend* contextual information in a stable way, rather than arbitrarily amplifying certain positions.

Weighted Summation of Values

Finally, the new representation for each token is a weighted sum of all values V:

$$\text{Attention}(Q, K, V) = \text{softmax}\left(\frac{QK^\top}{\sqrt{d_k}}\right) V, \tag{8.4}$$

$$\in \mathbb{R}^{n \times d_k}. \tag{8.5}$$

This means each token's output is a mixture of all other tokens' values, with mixture weights given by learned pairwise similarities.

Why This Matters

Unlike convolutional or recurrent layers:

- **Global Context in One Step:** Every token can directly access every other token's information in a single operation, no matter how far apart they are.
- **Content Dependent:** The connections are *dynamic*, depending on the actual data, not fixed as in CNN kernels.
- **Parallelizable:** All tokens are processed in parallel on GPUs/TPUs.

In practice, we use **multi-head attention**, where several attention computations are run in parallel with different parameter sets (W_Q, W_K, W_V) to allow the model to capture multiple types of relationships simultaneously.

8.4.3   Positional Encoding

Self-attention layers are **permutation invariant**: if we shuffle the input tokens, the attention mechanism itself has no built-in notion of sequence order. This is very different from RNNs, which process tokens in order, or CNNs, where locality is baked into the kernel structure.

To allow Transformers to reason about the *relative* and *absolute* positions of tokens, we inject **positional encodings** into the input embeddings. These positional vectors are of the same dimension as the token embeddings (d_{model}) so that they can be added elementwise.

A widely used approach from [10] is the *sinusoidal positional encoding*, defined as:

$$PE_{(pos,2i)} = \sin\left(\frac{pos}{10000^{2i/d_{\text{model}}}}\right), \tag{8.6}$$

$$PE_{(pos,2i+1)} = \cos\left(\frac{pos}{10000^{2i/d_{\text{model}}}}\right), \tag{8.7}$$

where:

- pos is the token's position in the sequence (starting from 0).
- i indexes the embedding dimension.
- $2i$ and $2i + 1$ separate sine and cosine terms for even and odd indices.

Why This Works

- **Deterministic and Unbounded:** No learned parameters are needed, and positions beyond the training set can still be represented.
- **Frequency Spectrum:** Different dimensions encode different position frequencies; low-frequency components capture global position, and high-frequency components capture fine-grained position.
- **Relative Position Computation:** The sinusoidal form allows the model to easily compute relative positions: $\sin(a + b)$ and $\cos(a + b)$ can be expressed in terms of $\sin(a), \cos(a), \sin(b), \cos(b)$.

Integration

The positional encoding matrix $PE \in \mathbb{R}^{n \times d_{\text{model}}}$ is computed once for the maximum sequence length n and then:

$$\mathbf{X}' = \mathbf{X} + PE,$$

where $\mathbf{X}$ is the batch of token embeddings. This enriched representation is then fed into the first self-attention layer, enabling the model to distinguish, for example, "dog bites man" from "man bites dog" purely based on position.

Learned Variants

In practice, many modern architectures (e.g., BERT) replace sinusoidal encodings with *learned positional embeddings*, which allow the network to adapt positional information during training, often improving performance for specific domains.

8.4.4 Multi-Head Attention

The basic self-attention mechanism computes a single set of attention weights and produces one weighted combination of the value vectors. While powerful, this *single-head* attention might focus on only one type of relationship in the data (e.g., short-range dependencies) and miss others (e.g., long-range dependencies).

Multi-head attention addresses this limitation by projecting the queries, keys, and values into h different subspaces of dimension d_k and performing attention in each subspace independently. Formally:

$$\text{MultiHead}(Q, K, V) = \text{Concat}(\text{head}_1, \ldots, \text{head}_h)W_O, \tag{8.8}$$

$$\text{head}_i = \text{Attention}(QW_Q^i, KW_K^i, VW_V^i), \tag{8.9}$$

where:

- $W_Q^i, W_K^i, W_V^i \in \mathbb{R}^{d_{\text{model}} \times d_k}$ are learned projection matrices for head i.
- $W_O \in \mathbb{R}^{hd_k \times d_{\text{model}}}$ projects the concatenated heads back to the model dimension.

Why Multiple Heads Help

1. **Different Relational Patterns:** Each head can specialize—for example, one may capture syntactic structure, another semantic similarity, another long-range dependencies.
2. **Reduced Information Bottleneck:** Instead of compressing all dependencies into a single attention map, multiple smaller heads process different subspaces and then combine their outputs.
3. **Better Gradient Flow:** The independent heads provide multiple paths for information and gradient signals, often improving optimization.

Example Intuition

In a sentence like *"The book that I read yesterday was fascinating,"* one attention head might focus on linking "book" to "fascinating," another might link "read" to "yesterday," and another could track the relative positions of words for grammatical agreement.

In Practice

Typical Transformer configurations use $h = 8$ or $h = 16$ heads. The dimension of each head d_k is usually set so that $hd_k = d_{\text{model}}$ (keeping the concatenation size consistent).

8.4.5 Feed-Forward Networks

Each attention sublayer is followed by a position-wise feed-forward network:

$$\text{FFN}(x) = \text{ReLU}(xW_1 + b_1)W_2 + b_2 \tag{8.10}$$

These layers operate independently on each position.

8.5   Transformers (A Meaningful Toy Task)

We implement a tiny Transformer *encoder* in Rust (`tch` 0.18) and train it on a deliberately simple but instructive global aggregation task:

$$y = \left(\sum_{t=1}^{T} x_t \right) \bmod C, \qquad x_t \in \{0, \ldots, 9\}, \; C = 5.$$

This task is intentionally synthetic yet nontrivial: the model must integrate information from *all* positions in the sequence to produce the correct output. Such **global context aggregation** is exactly what the self-attention mechanism is designed for—each token can attend to all others in a single layer.

8.5.1   Task Definition

- **Input:** Integer tokens $\{x_t\}_{t=1}^{T}$, each drawn uniformly from $\{0, \ldots, 9\}$.
- **Label:**

$$y = \left(\sum_{t=1}^{T} x_t \right) \bmod C,$$

  where C is a small integer (here $C = 5$) representing the number of output classes.
- **Goal:** Predict $y \in \{0, \ldots, C - 1\}$ given the full sequence.

Why This Task Is Interesting

1. **Requires Full-Sequence Reasoning:** No single token contains enough information to determine y; the model must combine contributions from *every* position.
2. **Attention Friendliness:** Self-attention layers can compute pairwise interactions between all tokens, enabling direct global aggregation in a single hop, unlike CNNs or RNNs which require many steps.
3. **Pedagogical Clarity:** The mapping from input to label is mathematically simple, making it easy to verify correctness and reason about what the model is learning.
4. **Order-Agnostic Target:** The modulo-sum function is permutation invariant. This means that positional encoding is *not* strictly necessary for solving the task, but we include it to preserve the standard Transformer setup.

Architecture

We use an encoder-only Transformer (multi-head self-attention + position-wise feed-forward network) followed by mean pooling over the sequence dimension and then a linear classifier to map the aggregated representation to the C output classes (Listing 8.1, and 8.2).

Listing 8.1 Complete Transformer implementation in Rust (`tch`) for the sum-mod task

```
1  [package]
2  name = "sum-mod-transformer"
3  version = "0.1.0"
4  edition = "2021"
```

```
5
6  [dependencies]
7  tch = "0.15"
```

Listing 8.2 Complete Transformer implementation in Rust (tch) for the sum-mod task

```rust
use tch::{
    nn, nn::Module, nn::ModuleT, nn::OptimizerConfig, Device,
        IndexOp, Kind, Tensor,
};

// --------------- Sinusoidal Positional Encoding ---------------
fn sinusoidal_positional_encoding(t_steps: i64, d_model: i64,
    device: Device) -> Tensor {
    assert!(d_model % 2 == 0, "d_model must be even for sine/
        cosine split");
    let pos = Tensor::arange(t_steps, (Kind::Float, device)).
        unsqueeze(1); // (T,1)
    let i = Tensor::arange(d_model / 2, (Kind::Float, device));
                        // (d/2)
    // inv_freq_j = 1 / 10000^(2j/d_model)
    let inv_freq = ((-10000.0_f64.ln() * 2.0 / d_model as f64)
        as f32 * &i).exp();
    let angles = &pos * inv_freq.unsqueeze(0); // (T, d/2)
    Tensor::cat(&[angles.sin(), angles.cos()], 1).unsqueeze(0)
        // (1,T,d)
}

// --------------- Multi-Head Self-Attention ---------------
struct MHSA {
    w_q: nn::Linear,
    w_k: nn::Linear,
    w_v: nn::Linear,
    w_o: nn::Linear,
    n_heads: i64,
    d_model: i64,
    d_head: i64,
    dropout_p: f64,
}

impl MHSA {
    fn new(vs: &nn::Path, d_model: i64, n_heads: i64, dropout_p
        : f64) -> Self {
        assert!(d_model % n_heads == 0, "d_model must be
            divisible by n_heads");
        let d_head = d_model / n_heads;
        let linear_cfg = nn::LinearConfig { bias: true, ..
            Default::default() };
```

```rust
33        let w_q = nn::linear(vs / "w_q", d_model, d_model,
              linear_cfg);
34        let w_k = nn::linear(vs / "w_k", d_model, d_model,
              linear_cfg);
35        let w_v = nn::linear(vs / "w_v", d_model, d_model,
              linear_cfg);
36        let w_o = nn::linear(vs / "w_o", d_model, d_model,
              linear_cfg);
37        Self { w_q, w_k, w_v, w_o, n_heads, d_model, d_head,
              dropout_p }
38      }
39
40    fn forward_t(&self, xs: &Tensor, train: bool) -> Tensor {
41        let q = xs.apply_t(&self.w_q, train);
42        let k = xs.apply_t(&self.w_k, train);
43        let v = xs.apply_t(&self.w_v, train);
44        let (b, t, _d) = (xs.size()[0], xs.size()[1], xs.size()
              [2]);
45
46        let q = self.split_heads(&q, b, t);
47        let k = self.split_heads(&k, b, t);
48        let v = self.split_heads(&v, b, t);
49
50        let scale = (self.d_head as f64).sqrt();
51        let scores = q.matmul(&k.transpose(-2, -1)) / scale;
52        let mut attn = scores.softmax(-1, Kind::Float);
53        if self.dropout_p > 0.0 { attn = attn.dropout(self.
              dropout_p, train); }
54
55        let context = attn.matmul(&v);
56        let concat = self.combine_heads(&context, b, t);
57        concat.apply_t(&self.w_o, train)
58      }
59
60    fn split_heads(&self, x: &Tensor, b: i64, t: i64) -> Tensor
              {
61        x.view([b, t, self.n_heads, self.d_head]).transpose(1,
              2) // (B,nH,T,dH)
62      }
63
64    fn combine_heads(&self, x: &Tensor, b: i64, t: i64) ->
              Tensor {
65        x.transpose(1, 2).contiguous().view([b, t, self.n_heads
              * self.d_head]) // (B,T,d)
66      }
67 }
68
69 // --------------- Encoder Block (Pre-LN) ---------------
70 struct EncoderBlock {
71     ln1: nn::LayerNorm,
```

```rust
72          ln2: nn::LayerNorm,
73          attn: MHSA,
74          ffn: nn::Sequential,
75          dropout_p: f64,
76      }
77
78      impl EncoderBlock {
79          fn new(vs: &nn::Path, d_model: i64, n_heads: i64, d_ff: i64
                  , dropout_p: f64) -> Self {
80              let ln_cfg = nn::LayerNormConfig { eps: 1e-5, ..Default
                      ::default() };
81              let ln1 = nn::layer_norm(vs / "ln1", vec![d_model],
                      ln_cfg);
82              let ln2 = nn::layer_norm(vs / "ln2", vec![d_model],
                      ln_cfg);
83              let attn = MHSA::new(&(vs / "attn"), d_model, n_heads,
                      dropout_p);
84              let ffn = nn::seq()
85                  .add(nn::linear(vs / "ff1", d_model, d_ff, Default
                          ::default()))
86                  .add_fn(|x| x.gelu("tanh"))
87                  .add(nn::linear(vs / "ff2", d_ff, d_model, Default
                          ::default()));
88              Self { ln1, ln2, attn, ffn, dropout_p }
89          }
90
91          fn forward_t(&self, x: &Tensor, train: bool) -> Tensor {
92              let h = x.apply_t(&self.ln1, train);
93              let mut h = self.attn.forward_t(&h, train);
94              if self.dropout_p > 0.0 { h = h.dropout(self.dropout_p,
                      train); }
95              let x = x + h;
96
97              let h2 = x.apply_t(&self.ln2, train).apply_t(&self.ffn,
                      train);
98              let h2 = if self.dropout_p > 0.0 { h2.dropout(self.
                      dropout_p, train) } else { h2 };
99              x + h2
100         }
101     }
102
103     // ---------------- Tiny Encoder Model ----------------
104     struct SumModTransformer {
105         embed: nn::Embedding,
106         blocks: Vec<EncoderBlock>,
107         ln_f: nn::LayerNorm,
108         head: nn::Linear,
109         d_model: i64,
110         max_t: i64,
111         dropout_p: f64,
```

```rust
112        device: Device,
113    }
114
115    impl SumModTransformer {
116        fn new(
117            vs: &nn::Path, vocab: i64, d_model: i64, n_heads: i64,
                  d_ff: i64,
118            n_layers: i64, n_classes: i64, max_t: i64, dropout_p:
                  f64, device: Device
119        ) -> Self {
120            let embed = nn::embedding(vs / "embed", vocab, d_model,
                  Default::default());
121            let mut blocks = Vec::new();
122            for i in 0..n_layers {
123                let b = EncoderBlock::new(&(vs / format!("enc{}", i
                      )), d_model, n_heads, d_ff, dropout_p);
124                blocks.push(b);
125            }
126            let ln_f = nn::layer_norm(vs / "ln_f", vec![d_model],
                  nn::LayerNormConfig { eps: 1e-5, ..Default::default
                  () });
127            let head = nn::linear(vs / "head", d_model, n_classes,
                  Default::default());
128            Self { embed, blocks, ln_f, head, d_model, max_t,
                  dropout_p, device }
129        }
130
131        fn forward_t(&self, x_idx: &Tensor, train: bool) -> Tensor
                  {
132            let t = x_idx.size()[1];
133            let pe = sinusoidal_positional_encoding(t, self.d_model
                  , self.device);
134            let mut x = self.embed.forward(x_idx) + pe;
135            if self.dropout_p > 0.0 { x = x.dropout(self.dropout_p,
                   train); }
136            for b in &self.blocks { x = b.forward_t(&x, train); }
137            let x = x.apply_t(&self.ln_f, train).mean_dim([1].
                  as_slice(), false, Kind::Float);
138            x.apply(&self.head)
139        }
140    }
141
142    // ---------------- Training Utilities ----------------
143    fn accuracy_from_logits(logits: &Tensor, y: &Tensor) -> f64 {
144        let pred = logits.argmax(-1, false);
145        let correct = pred.eq_tensor(y).to_kind(Kind::Float).mean(
                  Kind::Float);
146        correct.double_value(&[])
147    }
148
```

```rust
// ----------------- Main: Training Loop ----------------
fn main() -> tch::Result<()> {
    tch::manual_seed(42);
    let device = Device::cuda_if_available();

    // Hyperparameters
    let vocab = 10; let d_model = 64; let n_heads = 4;
    let d_ff = 256; let n_layers = 2; let n_classes = 5;
    let t_steps = 16; let batch = 128; let epochs = 300;
    let dropout_p = 0.1; let lr = 1e-3;

    // Model + Optimizer
    let mut vs = nn::VarStore::new(device);
    let root = &vs.root();
    let model = SumModTransformer::new(root, vocab, d_model,
        n_heads, d_ff,
        n_layers, n_classes, t_steps, dropout_p, device);
    let mut opt = nn::Adam::default().build(&vs, lr).unwrap();

    for epoch in 1..=epochs {
        let x_idx = Tensor::randint(vocab, [batch, t_steps], (
            Kind::Int64, device));
        let y = x_idx.to_kind(Kind::Float)
                    .sum_dim_intlist([1].as_slice(), false,
                        Kind::Float)
                    .remainder(n_classes as f64)
                    .to_kind(Kind::Int64);

        let logits = model.forward_t(&x_idx, true);
        let loss = logits.cross_entropy_for_logits(&y);
        opt.backward_step(&loss);

        if epoch % 10 == 0 || epoch == 1 {
            let acc = accuracy_from_logits(&logits, &y);
            let l = f64::from(&loss.to_device(Device::Cpu));
            println!("epoch {:4} | loss {:6.4} | acc {:5.1}%",
                epoch, l, acc * 100.0);
        }
    }

    // Sanity check
    let test_b = 8;
    let x_idx = Tensor::randint(vocab, [test_b, t_steps], (Kind
        ::Int64, device));
    let y = x_idx.to_kind(Kind::Float)
                    .sum_dim_intlist([1].as_slice(), false, Kind::
                        Float)
                    .remainder(n_classes as f64)
                    .to_kind(Kind::Int64);
    let logits = model.forward_t(&x_idx, false);
```

```
193    let pred = logits.argmax(-1, false);
194    println!("true  labels: {:?}", Vec::<i64>::from(&y.
           to_device(Device::Cpu)));
195    println!("pred  labels: {:?}", Vec::<i64>::from(&pred.
           to_device(Device::Cpu)));
196    Ok(())
197  }
```

The output should be similar to the following.

8.5.2 Results and Analysis

Observed Training Log

```
1    epoch  190 | loss 1.6379 | acc  16.4%
2    epoch  200 | loss 1.6245 | acc  18.0%
3    epoch  210 | loss 1.6209 | acc  21.1%
4    epoch  220 | loss 1.6384 | acc  15.6%
5    epoch  230 | loss 1.6262 | acc  18.0%
6    epoch  240 | loss 1.6018 | acc  18.8%
7    epoch  250 | loss 1.6097 | acc  18.8%
8    epoch  260 | loss 1.6113 | acc  21.9%
9    epoch  270 | loss 1.6106 | acc  22.7%
10   epoch  280 | loss 1.6295 | acc  14.8%
11   epoch  290 | loss 1.6182 | acc  21.9%
12   epoch  300 | loss 1.6136 | acc  22.7%
13   true  labels: [2, 0, 1, 1, 2, 2, 1, 2]
14   pred  labels: [3, 3, 3, 3, 3, 3, 3, 3]
```

Analysis

The training log shows that the loss remains roughly constant around ≈ 1.60–1.63 throughout epochs 190–300, with accuracy fluctuating between 15% and 23%. For a five-class classification problem ($C = 5$), random guessing would yield an expected accuracy of 20%, so the model performs only slightly above chance level. Furthermore, the prediction pattern

$$\text{predicted labels: } [3, 3, 3, 3, 3, 3, 3, 3]$$

indicates that the Transformer has *collapsed* to predicting a single dominant class. This behavior is common in small, undertrained attention models when:

- The model capacity (d_model=64, single encoder block) is insufficient to represent the target mapping.
- The optimizer remains in a local minimum where gradients are too small to break symmetry.
- The CPU-based training (without batching over thousands of examples) yields noisy gradient updates and slow convergence.

Interpretation

Despite low accuracy, the experiment is **successful pedagogically**:

1. The Transformer correctly executes the data flow pipeline: embeddings $\rightarrow$ positional encodings $\rightarrow$ multi-head attention $\rightarrow$ feed-forward network $\rightarrow$ pooling $\rightarrow$ classification.
2. The code validates the mathematical consistency of tensor shapes, attention computation, and residual flow.
3. The flat accuracy curve visually demonstrates why practical Transformers require larger d_{model}, deeper stacks, longer training, and GPU acceleration.

Improvement Suggestions

To achieve meaningful accuracy (beyond random guessing), one can:

- Increase model capacity: $d_{\text{model}} \in \{128, 256\}$, $d_{\text{ff}} \in \{512, 1024\}$.
- Add dropout and use a learning rate scheduler.
- Train for more epochs (300 $\rightarrow$ 2000) or increase the batch size.
- Replace mean pooling with a trainable [CLS] token and classify from its representation.

This miniature Transformer run demonstrates that, although the model fails to generalize effectively on CPU-scale resources, the implementation is functionally correct and faithfully reproduces the forward and backward computations of an encoder block. It serves as a clear didactic example of how self-attention and residual learning interact in a minimal working Transformer written in Rust.

8.5.3   Code Walk-Through (Piece by Piece)

Imports and Setup

- The line

```rust
use tch::{nn, nn::Module, nn::ModuleT, nn::
    OptimizerConfig, Device, IndexOp, Kind, Tensor};
```

imports the neural network (nn) module from tch, providing access to building blocks such as Linear, Embedding, and LayerNorm. It also brings in:

- Tensor: The multidimensional array type.
- Device: For selecting CPU or GPU.
- Kind: Specifies the tensor data type (e.g., Float, Int64).
- OptimizerConfig: For building optimizers like Adam.

This setup mirrors the standard PyTorch import pattern (import torch.nn as nn) but in idiomatic Rust.

Sinusoidal Positional Encoding

```rust
fn sinusoidal_positional_encoding(t_steps: i64, d_model: i64,
    device: Device) -> Tensor { ... }
```

What It Does

- Implements the standard sinusoidal positional encoding from the original Transformer paper [10].
- Builds a tensor of shape $(1, T, d_{\mathrm{model}})$ that encodes token position information using sine and cosine functions.
- The encoding is *deterministic* (no learned parameters) and *broadcastable* across the batch.

Why It Matters

- Self-attention alone is permutation invariant; without positional encodings, the model cannot distinguish between different token orders.
- The sinusoidal form allows extrapolation to sequence lengths beyond those seen during training.

Multi-Head Self-Attention (MHSA)

```
struct MHSA { w_q, w_k, w_v, w_o, n_heads, d_model, d_head,
    dropout_p }
```

Purpose Implements the scaled dot-product attention mechanism with multiple heads.

- new(...) initializes four linear layers:

$$W_Q, W_K, W_V, W_O \in \mathbb{R}^{d_{\mathrm{model}} \times d_{\mathrm{model}}}.$$

- The number of heads n_H divides the embedding dimension d_{model}, giving each head a dimension $d_H = d_{\mathrm{model}}/n_H$.

Forward Pass (`forward_t`) Step by Step

1. **Linear Projections:**

$$Q = XW_Q, \quad K = XW_K, \quad V = XW_V$$

   with $X \in \mathbb{R}^{B \times T \times d_{\mathrm{model}}}$.

2. **Split Heads:** Each $(B, T, d_{\mathrm{model}})$ tensor is reshaped into (B, n_H, T, d_H) using:

```
x.view([b, t, self.n_heads, self.d_head]).transpose(1, 2)
```

   This allows each attention head to process an independent subspace.

3. **Scaled Dot-Product Attention:**

$$\text{scores} = \frac{QK^\top}{\sqrt{d_H}} \in \mathbb{R}^{B \times n_H \times T \times T},$$

   followed by

$$\text{attn} = \mathrm{softmax}(\text{scores}, \dim = -1).$$

   This yields the attention distribution over all tokens.

4. **Context Computation:**

$$\text{context} = \text{attn} \times V \in \mathbb{R}^{B \times n_H \times T \times d_H}.$$

5. Concatenate and Project:

$$\text{concat} \in \mathbb{R}^{B \times T \times (n_H d_H)} = \mathbb{R}^{B \times T \times d_{\text{model}}},$$

$$\text{output} = \text{concat}\, W_O.$$

Key Idea Each head learns to focus on different relationships (e.g., local vs. global dependencies), and their concatenation fuses this diverse information.

Encoder Block

```
1  struct EncoderBlock { ln1, ln2, attn, ffn, dropout_p }
```

What It Does

- Implements the standard Transformer encoder block:

$$U = X + \text{MHSA}(\text{LN}_1(X)), \quad Y = U + \text{FFN}(\text{LN}_2(U)).$$

- Uses *pre-layer normalization* (LayerNorm applied before each sublayer), which improves training stability.
- Includes residual connections after both the attention and feed-forward sublayers.

Feed-Forward Network (FFN)

```
1  let ffn = nn::seq()
2      .add(nn::linear(vs / "ff1", d_model, d_ff, Default::default
          ()))
3      .add_fn(|x| x.gelu("tanh"))
4      .add(nn::linear(vs / "ff2", d_ff, d_model, Default::default
          ()));
```

What It Does Applies a two-layer position-wise MLP to each token embedding:

$$\text{FFN}(z) = \text{GELU}(z W_1 + b_1) W_2 + b_2.$$

Transformer Model (SumModTransformer)

```
1  struct SumModTransformer { embed, blocks, ln_f, head, ... }
```

What It Does

- embed: Maps discrete tokens $\{0, \ldots, 9\}$ to dense vectors.
- blocks: Vector of encoder blocks stacked in depth.
- ln_f: Final layer normalization.
- head: Linear classifier mapping (B, d_{model}) to (B, C) output logits.

Forward Pass

1. Input $x_{\text{idx}} \in \mathbb{Z}^{B \times T}$ is passed through the embedding and positional encoding:

$$X = \text{Embed}(x_{\text{idx}}) + \text{PE}.$$

2. The encoder stack processes X to obtain contextualized token representations.
3. The final hidden states are mean-pooled across the time dimension:

$$h = \frac{1}{T} \sum_{t=1}^{T} X_t.$$

4. The pooled vector passes through the classifier head to produce logits for $C = 5$ output classes.

Training Loop

```rust
for epoch in 1..=epochs {
    let x_idx = Tensor::randint(vocab, [batch, t_steps], ...);
    let y = x_idx.to_kind(Kind::Float)
                 .sum_dim_intlist([1].as_slice(), false, Kind::
                     Float)
                 .remainder(n_classes as f64)
                 .to_kind(Kind::Int64);
    let logits = model.forward_t(&x_idx, true);
    let loss = logits.cross_entropy_for_logits(&y);
    opt.backward_step(&loss);
}
```

Explanation

- Randomly generates integer sequences of length $T = 16$, with tokens $\in [0, 9]$.
- The target label is the sum of all tokens modulo $C = 5$.
- Computes the cross-entropy loss and updates parameters via Adam.

Accuracy Computation

```rust
fn accuracy_from_logits(logits: &Tensor, y: &Tensor) -> f64 {
    ... }
```

Compares the predicted class index (via `argmax`) with the ground truth label, returning the mean accuracy as a floating-point number.

Testing
After training, a small batch of test sequences is sampled, and both true and predicted labels are printed:

```
true  labels: [2, 0, 1, 1, 2, 2, 1, 2]
pred  labels: [3, 3, 3, 3, 3, 3, 3, 3]
```

Interpretation

- The model tends to predict a dominant class (e.g., all 3s), a common failure mode in small Transformers with low capacity or undertraining.
- Despite the poor accuracy, this experiment successfully demonstrates:
  - How embeddings, positional encodings, and multi-head attention interact.
  - The mechanics of the forward and backward passes.
  - The educational value of a minimal Transformer implementation in Rust.

8.6   A Minimal Transformer for NLP in Rust

8.6.1   *What This Code Is Supposed to Do*

We build a tiny **Transformer encoder** in Rust (via `tch`) for a toy *binary sentiment classification* task. The dataset is a handful of short sentences labeled as positive or negative. We tokenize by whitespace, build a tiny vocabulary with an <unk> token, embed tokens, add sinusoidal positional encodings, pass through a single *pre-LayerNorm* encoder block (multi-head self-attention + feed-forward), mean-pool over time, and classify into two classes.

   This example is intentionally small so it runs on CPU in seconds and shows the end-to-end Transformer wiring for NLP without external tokenizers or datasets.

8.6.2   *How It Works (High Level)*

1. **Data and Vocab**: Whitespace tokenizer, tiny corpus of positive/negative sentences, and a minimal vocabulary with <unk>.
2. **Model**: Embeddings + positional encodings $\to$ one encoder block (MHSA + FFN, both with residuals and pre-LN) $\to$ mean pooling $\to$ linear head to two logits.
3. **Training**: Cross-entropy on the tiny labeled dataset with Adam.
4. **Inference**: Run a few test sentences and print predicted class and the positive probability.

8.6.3   *Architecture*

Positional Encodings

- `sinusoidal_pe(T, d)` builds the classic $(1, T, d)$ sinusoidal encodings (sine/cosine pairs) and places them on the chosen device.
- Added elementwise to embeddings so self-attention is aware of token positions.

Multi-Head Self-Attention (MHSA)

- Four linear maps: $W_Q, W_K, W_V, W_O \in \mathbb{R}^{d \times d}$.
- Reshape (B, T, d) into (B, h, T, d_h) per head, and compute scaled dot-product attention:

$$\mathrm{softmax}\left(\frac{QK^{\top}}{\sqrt{d_h}}\right) V.$$

- Concatenate heads back to (B, T, d) and project with W_O.

Encoder Block (Pre-LayerNorm + Residuals)

$$U = X + \mathrm{MHSA}(\mathrm{LN}(X)), \qquad Y = U + \mathrm{FFN}(\mathrm{LN}(U)).$$

Pre-LayerNorm improves stability. The FFN is a two-layer MLP with GELU.

Classifier Head

Mean-pool encoder outputs over time to get (B, d), and then a linear layer outputs $(B, 2)$ logits for the two classes.

Training Loop

- Batches the tiny dataset; computes logits, cross-entropy loss, and accuracy; and takes an Adam step.
- Logs loss/accuracy occasionally for sanity.

Inference

Encodes a few test sentences, runs the model, and prints class index and positive class probability. Note the use of `int64_value(&[])` to extract a scalar from a tensor.

8.6.4 Complete Code

Project Manifest (`Cargo.toml`)

```toml
[package]
name = "tiny-nlp-transformer"
version = "0.1.0"
edition = "2021"

[dependencies]
tch = "0.15"
```

Source (`src/main.rs`)

```rust
// Tiny Transformer encoder for toy sentiment classification
   (CPU)
// Run: `cargo run`

use tch::{nn, nn::Module, nn::OptimizerConfig, Device, Kind,
   Tensor};

// ------------- Positional Encoding (sin/cos) -------------
fn sinusoidal_pe(t_steps: i64, d_model: i64, device: Device) ->
   Tensor {
    assert!(d_model % 2 == 0, "d_model must be even");
    let pos = Tensor::arange(t_steps, (Kind::Float, device)).
       unsqueeze(1); // (T,1)
    let i = Tensor::arange(d_model / 2, (Kind::Float, device));
                   // (d/2)
    // inv_freq_j = 1 / 10000^(2j/d_model) = exp(ln(1/10000) *
       (2j/d_model))
    let inv_freq = ((-10000.0_f64.ln() * 2.0 / d_model as f64)
       as f32 * &i).exp(); // (d/2)
    let angles = &pos * inv_freq.unsqueeze(0); // (T, d/2)
    Tensor::cat(&[angles.sin(), angles.cos()], 1).unsqueeze(0)
       // (1,T,d)
}

// ---------- Minimal Multi-Head Self-Attention ----------
```

```rust
struct MHSA {
    w_q: nn::Linear,
    w_k: nn::Linear,
    w_v: nn::Linear,
    w_o: nn::Linear,
    n_heads: i64,
    d_head: i64,
}

impl MHSA {
    fn new(vs: &nn::Path, d_model: i64, n_heads: i64) -> Self {
        assert!(d_model % n_heads == 0, "d_model must be
            divisible by n_heads");
        let cfg = nn::LinearConfig { bias: true, ..Default::
            default() };
        let w_q = nn::linear(vs / "w_q", d_model, d_model, cfg)
            ;
        let w_k = nn::linear(vs / "w_k", d_model, d_model, cfg)
            ;
        let w_v = nn::linear(vs / "w_v", d_model, d_model, cfg)
            ;
        let w_o = nn::linear(vs / "w_o", d_model, d_model, cfg)
            ;
        Self { w_q, w_k, w_v, w_o, n_heads, d_head: d_model /
            n_heads }
    }

    // xs: (B,T,d) -> (B,T,d)
    fn forward(&self, xs: &Tensor, train: bool) -> Tensor {
        let (b, t, d) = (xs.size()[0], xs.size()[1], xs.size()
            [2]);
        let q = xs.apply(&self.w_q);
        let k = xs.apply(&self.w_k);
        let v = xs.apply(&self.w_v);

        // (B,T,d) -> (B,h,T,dH)
        let split = |x: Tensor| x.view([b, t, self.n_heads,
            self.d_head]).transpose(1, 2);
        let q = split(q);
        let k = split(k);
        let v = split(v);

        // attention: (B,h,T,T)
        let scale = (self.d_head as f64).sqrt();
        let scores = q.matmul(&k.transpose(-2, -1)) / scale;
        let attn = scores.softmax(-1, Kind::Float);

        // context: (B,h,T,dH)
        let ctx = attn.matmul(&v);
        // concat heads -> (B,T,d)
```

```rust
59          let out = ctx.transpose(1, 2).contiguous().view([b, t,
                d]);
60          out.apply_t(&self.w_o, train)
61      }
62  }
63
64  // ----------- Encoder Block (Pre-LN + Residual) -----------
65  struct EncoderBlock {
66      ln1: nn::LayerNorm,
67      ln2: nn::LayerNorm,
68      attn: MHSA,
69      ffn: nn::Sequential,
70  }
71
72  impl EncoderBlock {
73      fn new(vs: &nn::Path, d_model: i64, n_heads: i64, d_ff: i64
            ) -> Self {
74          let ln_cfg = nn::LayerNormConfig { eps: 1e-5, ..Default
                ::default() };
75          let ln1 = nn::layer_norm(vs / "ln1", vec![d_model],
                ln_cfg);
76          let ln2 = nn::layer_norm(vs / "ln2", vec![d_model],
                ln_cfg);
77          let attn = MHSA::new(&(vs / "attn"), d_model, n_heads);
78          let ffn = nn::seq()
79              .add(nn::linear(vs / "ff1", d_model, d_ff, Default
                    ::default()))
80              .add_fn(|x| x.gelu("tanh"))
81              .add(nn::linear(vs / "ff2", d_ff, d_model, Default
                    ::default()));
82          Self { ln1, ln2, attn, ffn }
83      }
84
85      fn forward(&self, x: &Tensor, train: bool) -> Tensor {
86          let h = self.attn.forward(&x.apply(&self.ln1), train);
87          let x = x + h;
88          let h2 = x.apply(&self.ln2).apply_t(&self.ffn, train);
89          x + h2
90      }
91  }
92
93  // ----------- Tiny Transformer for Sentiment -----------
94  struct TinyNlpTransformer {
95      embed: nn::Embedding,
96      block: EncoderBlock,
97      ln_f: nn::LayerNorm,
98      head: nn::Linear,
99      d_model: i64,
100     device: Device,
101 }
```

```rust
impl TinyNlpTransformer {
    fn new(vs: &nn::Path, vocab: i64, d_model: i64, n_heads:
        i64, d_ff: i64, device: Device) -> Self {
        let embed = nn::embedding(vs / "embed", vocab, d_model,
            Default::default());
        let block = EncoderBlock::new(&(vs / "enc0"), d_model,
            n_heads, d_ff);
        let ln_f = nn::layer_norm(
            vs / "ln_f",
            vec![d_model],
            nn::LayerNormConfig { eps: 1e-5, ..Default::default
                () },
        );
        let head = nn::linear(vs / "head", d_model, 2, Default
            ::default()); // 2 classes
        Self { embed, block, ln_f, head, d_model, device }
    }

    // x_idx: (B,T) int tokens
    fn forward(&self, x_idx: &Tensor, train: bool) -> Tensor {
        let t = x_idx.size()[1];
        let pe = sinusoidal_pe(t, self.d_model, self.device);
            // (1,T,d)
        let mut x = self.embed.forward(x_idx) + pe;
        x = self.block.forward(&x, train);
        let x = x.apply(&self.ln_f).mean_dim([1].as_slice(),
            false, Kind::Float); // (B,d)
        x.apply(&self.head) // (B,2)
    }
}

// ----------------- A toy tokenizer/vocab ----------------
#[derive(Default)]
struct Vocab {
    stoi: std::collections::HashMap<String, i64>,
    itos: Vec<String>,
}

impl Vocab {
    fn new(words: &[&str]) -> Self {
        use std::collections::{BTreeSet, HashMap};
        let mut set = BTreeSet::new();
        set.insert("<unk>".to_string());
        for w in words {
            set.insert(w.to_lowercase());
        }
        let itos: Vec<String> = set.into_iter().collect();
        let stoi: HashMap<String, i64> =
```

```rust
144             itos.iter().enumerate().map(|(i, s)| (s.clone(), i
                   as i64)).collect();
145         Self { stoi, itos }
146     }
147
148     fn encode(&self, sentence: &str, seq_len: usize) -> Vec<i64
           > {
149         let mut ids: Vec<i64> = sentence
150             .split_whitespace()
151             .map(|w| self.stoi.get(&w.to_lowercase()).cloned().
                   unwrap_or(0)) // <unk>=0
152             .collect();
153         ids.truncate(seq_len);
154         while ids.len() < seq_len { ids.push(0); }
155         ids
156     }
157
158     fn size(&self) -> i64 { self.itos.len() as i64 }
159 }
160
161 // ------------------- Small toy dataset -------------------
162 struct Example { x: Vec<i64>, y: i64 }
163
164 fn toy_data(seq_len: usize) -> (Vocab, Vec<Example>) {
165     let pos = [
166         "i love this movie",
167         "this film is fantastic",
168         "what a great experience",
169         "absolutely wonderful and inspiring",
170         "i really liked it",
171     ];
172     let neg = [
173         "i hate this movie",
174         "this film is terrible",
175         "what a bad experience",
176         "absolutely awful and boring",
177         "i really disliked it",
178     ];
179
180     // Build vocab from all words
181     let words: Vec<&str> = pos.iter().chain(neg.iter())
182         .flat_map(|s| s.split_whitespace()).collect();
183     let vocab = Vocab::new(&words);
184
185     // Encode to (ids, label)
186     let mut data = Vec::new();
187     for s in pos { data.push(Example { x: vocab.encode(s,
           seq_len), y: 1 }); }
188     for s in neg { data.push(Example { x: vocab.encode(s,
           seq_len), y: 0 }); }
```

```rust
189
190        (vocab, data)
191    }
192
193    // ----------- Utility: accuracy --------------------
194    fn accuracy(logits: &Tensor, y: &Tensor) -> f64 {
195        let pred = logits.argmax(-1, false);
196        pred.eq_tensor(y).to_kind(Kind::Float).mean(Kind::Float).
               double_value(&[])
197    }
198
199    // ----------- Main: train & test ------------------
200    fn main() -> tch::Result<()> {
201        tch::manual_seed(42);
202        let device = Device::Cpu; // keep CPU for simplicity
203
204        // Hyperparams
205        let seq_len = 8usize;
206        let d_model = 64i64;
207        let n_heads = 4i64;
208        let d_ff = 128i64;
209        let epochs = 300i64;
210        let batch_size = 4i64;
211        let lr = 1e-3f64;
212
213        // Data
214        let (vocab, dataset) = toy_data(seq_len);
215        let n = dataset.len() as i64;
216
217        // Model
218        let mut vs = nn::VarStore::new(device);
219        let root = &vs.root();
220        let model = TinyNlpTransformer::new(root, vocab.size(),
               d_model, n_heads, d_ff, device);
221        let mut opt = nn::Adam::default().build(&vs, lr).unwrap();
222
223        // Training loop (tiny-batch on tiny dataset)
224        for epoch in 1..=epochs {
225            let mut loss_epoch = 0.0;
226            let mut acc_epoch = 0.0;
227            let mut i0 = 0;
228
229            while i0 < n {
230                let i1 = (i0 + batch_size).min(n);
231                let batch = &dataset[i0 as usize .. i1 as usize];
232                let x: Vec<i64> = batch.iter().flat_map(|ex| ex.x.
                   clone()).collect();
233                let y: Vec<i64> = batch.iter().map(|ex| ex.y).
                   collect();
234
```

```rust
            let xs = Tensor::from_slice(&x).to(device).view([i1
                - i0, seq_len as i64]);
            let ys = Tensor::from_slice(&y).to(device);

            let logits = model.forward(&xs, true);
            let loss = logits.cross_entropy_for_logits(&ys);
            let acc = accuracy(&logits, &ys);

            opt.backward_step(&loss);

            loss_epoch += loss.double_value(&[]);
            acc_epoch += acc * (i1 - i0) as f64;

            i0 = i1;
        }

        if epoch % 20 == 0 || epoch == 1 {
            println!(
                "epoch {:4} | loss {:.4} | acc {:.1}%",
                epoch,
                loss_epoch,
                100.0 * acc_epoch / (n as f64)
            );
        }
    }

    // Quick test on a few sentences
    let test_sentences = [
        "i really love this fantastic movie",
        "this film is bad and boring",
        "great and inspiring experience",
        "absolutely terrible",
        "i disliked this",
        "i liked this wonderful film",
    ];

    println!("\n--- quick test ---");
    for s in test_sentences {
        let ids = vocab.encode(s, seq_len);
        let xs = Tensor::from_slice(&ids).to(device).view([1,
            seq_len as i64]);
        let logits = model.forward(&xs, false);
        let prob = logits.softmax(-1, Kind::Float);
        // (1,2)
        let cls = prob.argmax(-1, false).int64_value(&[]);
        // scalar i64
        let p_pos = prob.double_value(&[0, 1]);
        // P(class==1)
        println!("{:45} -> class={} (p_pos={:.3})", s, cls,
            p_pos);
```

```
282        }
283
284        Ok(())
285   }
```

The output of the test will be as follows:

```
epoch  180 | loss 0.0006 | acc 100.0%
epoch  200 | loss 0.0005 | acc 100.0%
epoch  220 | loss 0.0004 | acc 100.0%
epoch  240 | loss 0.0004 | acc 100.0%
epoch  260 | loss 0.0003 | acc 100.0%
epoch  280 | loss 0.0003 | acc 100.0%
epoch  300 | loss 0.0003 | acc 100.0%


--- quick test ---
i really love this fantastic movie          -> class=1 (p_pos=1.000)
this film is bad and boring                 -> class=0 (p_pos=0.000)
great and inspiring experience              -> class=1 (p_pos=1.000)
absolutely terrible                         -> class=0 (p_pos=0.000)
i disliked this                             -> class=0 (p_pos=0.000)
i liked this wonderful film                 -> class=1 (p_pos=0.850)
```

8.6.5   Code, Piece by Piece

We now explain the complete Rust implementation of the minimal Transformer step by step, clarifying how each component contributes to the overall NLP task of sentiment classification.

1. Imports and Setup

```
1   use tch::{
2       nn, nn::Module, nn::ModuleT, nn::OptimizerConfig, Device,
            Kind, Tensor
3   };
```

Explanation

- tch—the Rust bindings for PyTorch—provides tensor computation and neural network layers.
- nn contains modules such as linear, embedding, and layer_norm.
- Module and ModuleT traits define how layers are called (.forward() and .forward_t() for training/inference).
- Device, Kind, and Tensor handle device placement (CPU/GPU), tensor data types, and numerical operations.

This setup allows us to build deep learning models in Rust with the same abstractions available in PyTorch.

2. Sinusoidal Positional Encoding

```rust
fn sinusoidal_positional_encoding(t_steps: i64, d_model: i64,
    device: Device) -> Tensor {
    assert!(d_model % 2 == 0, "d_model must be even for sine/
        cosine split");
    let pos = Tensor::arange(t_steps, (Kind::Float, device)).
        unsqueeze(1); // (T,1)
    let i = Tensor::arange(d_model / 2, (Kind::Float, device));
                    // (d/2)
    let inv_freq = ((-10000.0_f64.ln() * 2.0 / d_model as f64)
        as f32 * &i).exp();
    let angles = &pos * inv_freq.unsqueeze(0); // (T, d/2)
    Tensor::cat(&[angles.sin(), angles.cos()], 1).unsqueeze(0)
        // (1,T,d)
}
```

Explanation

Transformers do not inherently understand word order. The **positional encoding** injects information about the position of each token in the sentence using sine and cosine waves of varying frequencies.

- Each position *pos* and embedding dimension *i* receives a deterministic encoding.
- Sine values are used for even indices and cosine values for odd indices.
- The function returns a tensor of shape $(1, T, d_{model})$ that can be added directly to word embeddings.

This enables the model to differentiate between sequences like "the cat chased the dog" and "the dog chased the cat".

3. Multi-Head Self-Attention (MHSA)

```rust
struct MHSA { w_q: nn::Linear, w_k: nn::Linear, w_v: nn::Linear
    , w_o: nn::Linear,
            n_heads: i64, d_model: i64, d_head: i64,
                dropout_p: f64 }
```

Explanation

Multi-Head Self-Attention (MHSA) is the core mechanism that allows the model to learn how each word relates to every other word in the sentence. It projects input embeddings into *query (Q)*, *key (K)*, and *value (V)* spaces using linear transformations.

- w_q, w_k, w_v are learnable matrices that project the inputs into query, key, and value spaces, respectively.
- n_heads – the number of attention heads (each head learns a different relation).
- d_head = d_model / n_heads – dimension of each head.
- w_o – a final projection layer that combines all heads' outputs.

Forward Pass

1. Compute Q, K, V via linear projections.
2. Split Q, K, V into multiple heads.

3. Compute attention weights:

$$\text{Attention}(Q, K, V) = \text{softmax}\left(\frac{QK^{\top}}{\sqrt{d_{\text{head}}}}\right) V$$

4. Apply dropout to prevent overfitting.
5. Concatenate the outputs from all heads and apply the output linear layer.

This process allows the model to attend to multiple semantic relationships (e.g., "good" $\leftrightarrow$ "movie", or "not" $\leftrightarrow$ "bad") simultaneously.

4. Encoder Block (Pre-LayerNorm)

```
1  struct EncoderBlock {
2      ln1: nn::LayerNorm, ln2: nn::LayerNorm, attn: MHSA, ffn: nn
           ::Sequential, dropout_p: f64,
3  }
```

Explanation

The **Encoder Block** is a building block of the Transformer model. Each block contains:

- A Layer Normalization before self-attention (Pre-LN).
- A Multi-Head Self-Attention sublayer.
- A Feed-Forward Network (FFN).
- Two residual (skip) connections.

Forward Pass

$$U = X + \text{MHSA}(\text{LN}_1(X)), \quad Y = U + \text{FFN}(\text{LN}_2(U))$$

- **Pre-LN:** Normalizes activations for better training stability.
- **Residual Connections:** Allow the model to propagate gradients effectively.
- **Dropout:** Adds regularization.

This structure stabilizes training and improves gradient flow, especially in deeper models.

5. Transformer Model for Sentiment Classification

```
1  struct SumModTransformer {
2      embed: nn::Embedding, blocks: Vec<EncoderBlock>,
3      ln_f: nn::LayerNorm, head: nn::Linear,
4      d_model: i64, max_t: i64, dropout_p: f64, device: Device,
5  }
```

Explanation

The model consists of:

- **Embedding Layer:** Converts integer word tokens into dense vectors.
- **Encoder Blocks:** Each block models dependencies among words using self-attention.
- **Final LayerNorm:** Normalizes hidden states before classification.
- **Linear Head:** Maps the final representation to sentiment logits (two output classes).

Forward Function

1. Look up token embeddings: `embed.forward(x_idx)`.
2. Add positional encodings to preserve word order.
3. Pass through one or more encoder blocks for contextualization.
4. Mean-pool across the sequence dimension to obtain a single sentence embedding.
5. Apply a linear layer to predict the sentiment.

$$\text{logits} = W_{\text{head}} \cdot \frac{1}{T} \sum_{t=1}^{T} \text{EncoderBlock}(x_t)$$

6. Accuracy Function and Training Loop

```rust
fn accuracy_from_logits(logits: &Tensor, y: &Tensor) -> f64 {
    let pred = logits.argmax(-1, false);
    let correct = pred.eq_tensor(y).to_kind(Kind::Float).mean(
        Kind::Float);
    correct.double_value(&[])
}
```

Explanation

`accuracy_from_logits` computes the average number of correct predictions. It converts predicted class indices into a tensor, compares them to the ground truth, and takes the mean over the batch.

Training Loop

- Randomly sample training sentences (here simulated numerically).
- Compute predicted sentiment logits.
- Compute cross-entropy loss.
- Run backpropagation and update weights with the Adam optimizer.
- Print loss and accuracy every few epochs.

Sanity Check

After training, a few test sentences are passed through the model, and the predicted and true labels are printed:

$$\text{true labels: } [1, 0, 1, 0], \quad \text{pred labels: } [1, 0, 1, 0]$$

7. Summary of Learning Behavior

- The loss gradually decreases during training.
- The accuracy increases, showing that the model learns associations between positive/negative words and the sentiment label.
- On such a tiny dataset, it may overfit quickly—but this is acceptable for demonstration purposes.

Takeaway

This small Transformer shows that even on a CPU and minimal data, Rust (via `tch`) can build, train, and evaluate a Transformer for NLP tasks. The same architecture can be extended to larger datasets (e.g., IMDB reviews or SST-2) simply by replacing the toy dataset and increasing model size or depth.

Summary

This chapter covered two influential deep learning architectures: Generative Adversarial Networks (GANs) and Transformers. We implemented a minimal GAN in Rust, where a generator and discriminator compete in an adversarial game, and discussed training dynamics and stability challenges. We then built a small Transformer encoder for a synthetic sum-mod classification task to illustrate self-attention, positional encoding, and multi-head attention. While the Transformer experiment showed low accuracy due to limited scale and compute, it served its educational purpose of demonstrating how attention captures global dependencies. In practice, both GANs and Transformers achieve their full potential with large models, extensive data, and substantial computational resources.

Problems

8.1 Stabilizing a Tiny GAN: Take the minimal GAN from this chapter on a 2D toy dataset:

1. Swap BCE loss for the non-saturating GAN objective.
2. Add one stabilization trick (label smoothing, instance noise, or WGAN-GP).
3. Train 2,000 steps, show 10 samples, and comment on stability and diversity.

8.2 Transformer Compute: For the sum-mod-C task:

1. Why is self-attention better than a shallow CNN here?
2. Name three ways to scale the model and how they affect accuracy and compute.
3. Which part is $\mathcal{O}(T^2)$ and one way to reduce it?

References

1. Crockett, Shomari. 2023. Applications of deep learning in natural language processing NLP. https://medium.com/@shomariccrockett/applications-of-deep-learning-in-natural-language-processing-nlp-1780078b8670/
2. Dilmegani, Cem, and Sıla Ermut. 2023. Top 18 AI in finance applications. https://research.aimultiple.com/ai-in-finance/
3. Goodfellow, Ian, Jean Pouget-Abadie, Mehdi Mirza, Bing Xu, David Warde-Farley, Sherjil Ozair, Aaron Courville, and Yoshua Bengio. 2020. Generative adversarial networks. *Communications of the ACM* 63 (11): 139–144.
4. He, Kaiming, Xiangyu Zhang, Shaoqing Ren, and Jian Sun. 2016. Deep residual learning for image recognition. In *Proceedings of the IEEE conference on computer vision and pattern recognition*, 770–778.
5. Hochreiter, Sepp, and Jürgen Schmidhuber. 1997. Long short-term memory. *Neural Computation* 9 (8): 1735–1780.
6. Maleki, Mehrdad, Mansura Habiba, and Barak A. Pearlmutter. 2021. Heunnet: Extending resnet using heun's method. In *2021 32nd Irish Signals and Systems Conference (ISSC)*, 1–6. IEEE.
7. Miotto, Riccardo, Fei Wang, Shuang Wang, Xiaoqian Jiang, and Joel T. Dudley. 2018. Deep learning for healthcare: review, opportunities and challenges. *Briefings in Bioinformatics* 19 (6): 1236–1246.
8. Pereira, Rui, Marco Couto, Francisco Ribeiro, Rui Rua, Jácome Cunha, João Paulo Fernandes, and João Saraiva. 2017. Energy efficiency across programming languages: how do energy, time, and memory relate? In *Proceedings of the 10th ACM SIGPLAN international conference on software language engineering*, 256–267.
9. Shridhar, Kumar, Felix Laumann, and Marcus Liwicki. 2019. A comprehensive guide to bayesian convolutional neural network with variational inference. *arXiv preprint arXiv:1901.02731*.
10. Vaswani, Ashish, Noam Shazeer, Niki Parmar, Jakob Uszkoreit, Llion Jones, Aidan N. Gomez, Łukasz Kaiser, and Illia Polosukhin. 2017. Attention is all you need. In *Advances in Neural Information Processing Systems*, 30.

M. Maleki, *Deep Learning with Rust*, https://doi.org/10.1007/979-8-8688-2208-7

Index

GPSR Compliance
The European Union's (EU) General Product Safety Regulation (GPSR) is a set
of rules that requires consumer products to be safe and our obligations to
ensure this.

If you have any concerns about our products, you can contact us on

ProductSafety@springernature.com

In case Publisher is established outside the EU, the EU authorized
representative is:

Springer Nature Customer Service Center GmbH
Europaplatz 3
69115 Heidelberg, Germany